MATTHEW ARNOLD
AND THE DECLINE OF
ENGLISH ROMANTICISM

Oxford University Press, Amen House, London E.C.4

GLASGOW   NEW YORK   TORONTO   MELBOURNE   WELLINGTON
BOMBAY   CALCUTTA   MADRAS   KARACHI   KUALA LUMPUR
CAPE TOWN   IBADAN   NAIROBI   ACCRA

MATTHEW ARNOLD
AND THE DECLINE OF
ENGLISH ROMANTICISM

BY

D. G. JAMES

OXFORD
AT THE CLARENDON PRESS
1961

PRINTED IN GREAT BRITAIN

TO
GWYN AND ALICE

FOREWORD

THIS book consists of lectures which were delivered on the Gregynog Foundation at the University College of Wales, Aberystwyth, in April 1959. I take this opportunity of expressing to the Principal and Senate of the College my gratitude for their kind invitation to me to occupy a lectureship in which I had so many distinguished predecessors; and I express also my thanks for the hospitality and kindness which I received at the College during my stay there.

I trust I may add a word concerning the scope and purpose of the pages which follow: it is rarely easy to find a title which can fairly claim to be an accurate guide to what follows it. After trying, in the first lecture, to give as clear an impression as I could of the temperament of Arnold, I set myself in the last two lectures to illustrate the decline of Romanticism in England by reviewing Arnold's critical writings in the light of an exposition, in the second lecture, of what I take to be the perennial essence, purified from temporary accretions, of Romanticism. It would have been agreeable to me to take Arnold's poetry into the scope of my lectures; but although something is said of the poetry, a critical study of it does not find a place here. What I wished chiefly to do I judged that I was able to do by reviewing Arnold's criticism and critical doctrines. It will be seen that I think that Arnold's critical writings fall into barely concealed incoherence; but I was less anxious to criticize a great Victorian (from the safety of a hundred years gone by) than to exhibit as clearly as I could the great issues which baffled Arnold and which baffle us still more today.

The composition of lectures too often gives to what one writes a certain dogmatic and definitive air; and I am conscious that I have not escaped this in what follows. I would have liked to rewrite what I have written in the form of what might properly be called an essay, having a more discursive and exploratory manner. But lack of time has forbidden this. In any case, I was required by the conditions of appointment to the Gregynog Lectureship to publish the lectures; and it is a pleasure to comply with the letter, as well as the spirit, of the requirements of such generous hosts.

I add that in my second lecture, in section 3, I have drawn upon my British Academy Warton Lecture of 1950, *Wordsworth and Tennyson*.

Finally, I wish to express my thanks to Miss Sheila M. Evans for her expert typing of a difficult manuscript; and to Roger Sharrock for some last-minute help.

D. G. J.

University of Southampton
January, 1960

CONTENTS

1

THE TEMPERAMENT OF
MATTHEW ARNOLD

I

MATTHEW ARNOLD went into residence at Balliol on the 15 October 1841. The opening of the school year at Rugby had been delayed on account of fever in the town; it was late in September before the Arnolds left Fox How, their home in the Lakes, for Rugby. But the anxiety and inconvenience during September had been made endurable by the delight of Thomas Arnold at his appointment in August, by one of the last acts of Lord Melbourne before leaving office, to the Regius Chair of Modern History at Oxford. There had been no doubt in his mind about accepting it. He had had 'an earnest longing to have some direct connexion with Oxford' and 'visions of Bagley Wood and Shotover' had risen upon him 'with an irresistible charm'. When, therefore, Matthew went to Oxford, where in due course he would see Bagley Wood as one of the haunts of the Scholar Gypsy, it was to a University in which his father was to be a professor. But not only to be a professor; to be, as well, a hammer of the Tractarians.

Matthew seems to have had no clear notion about a

career when he went to Oxford. He had never applied himself to work with great ardour; and his father said of him before he went to Oxford that 'he likes general society, and flitters about from flower to flower, but is not apt to fix'. In a letter written in September 1841, Dr. Arnold said to a clergyman friend that he would be well pleased if one of his sons 'went out hereafter to labour in the same field [the Church], but what line they will take seems very hard to determine. They do not seem inclined to follow Medicine, and I have the deepest horror of the Law, so that two professions seem set aside, and for trade, I have neither capital nor connexion. Meanwhile, I wish them to do well at the University, which will be an arming them in a manner for whatever may open to them'. In fact, Matthew's business in life, like his father's, was to be education; and the more one reads in and about the two men, the more inevitable this seems to have been. But if Matthew went up to Oxford with no clear-cut schemes of work at the University and afterwards, his father was quick to lay down *his* plans. He would go up to deliver his inaugural lecture in the Michaelmas term, and his first course in the Lent. He gave his inaugural lecture on 2 December. He could not be away from Rugby for more than a day. He left Rugby very early and in darkness, marked school exercises when daylight came, and reached Oxford at noon. It had not been easy to find a lecture room that would contain the large crowd that would wish to hear him. The Clarendon Theatre was filled by it; and there, in the presence of the University authorities, in Tractarian Oxford, the strongest single antagonist in England of the Tractarian Movement declared that there was no privilege which he more valued, no public reward or honour which could be to him more welcome, than to address that audience 'as one of the Professors of Oxford'.

I said that there had been no doubt in his mind about accepting the Oxford chair. It is true that he had written to A. P. Stanley in the March of 1841 having in mind the Tractarian Movement: 'My own desire of going to Oxford was, as you know, long cherished and strong, but it is quenched now; I could not go to a place where I once lived so happily and so peaceably, and gained so much—to feel either constant and active enmity to the prevailing party in it—or else, by use and personal humanities, to become first tolerant of such monstrous evil, and then perhaps learn to sympathise with it.' But only six months earlier he had told J. T. Coleridge: 'But Oxford, both for its good and its beauty, which I love so tenderly, and for the evil now tainting it, which I would fain resist at its very birthplace, is the place where I would fain pass my latest years of unimpaired faculties'; and the desire to resist Tractarianism in its home, along with the irresistible charm of the Oxford country-side, proved easily stronger than dislike of the situation he foresaw. Therefore the occasion of his inaugural lecture inaugurated more than the tenure of a chair by a notable historian. The scene was set with Arnold and Newman standing over against each other for a great combat of ideas. They met on 2 February

1842: Arnold was spending the first three weeks of the Lent term at Oxford and delivered then his first course of lectures; and on 2 February he dined in Hall at Oriel. Knowing that Arnold would be there, Newman had thought to avoid dining that night; but in the end he decided he must go. He was already at table when the Provost brought Arnold in. One can sympathize with the Provost: he put on a brisk air to cover his embarrassment, and said, 'Arnold, I don't think you know Newman'. Newman put on a calm, unconcerned, innocent manner; Arnold was 'natural and easy'. They talked about vastly indifferent subjects. They certainly could not talk about Oxford; and a good deal of time went in talking about the natural history of North Africa, in particular of a tree reputed to be as big as a mountain.[1]

II

The year 1841 had been momentous in the history of the Tractarian party, and indeed of the University as a whole. On 27 February Tract 90 was published, and it was met with alarm and anger. On 13 March the Board of the Heads of Houses pronounced their judgement on it; and from then on it was clear that, as Dean Church said, 'the fate of the [Tractarian] party at Oxford was determined. . . . Sooner or later there must be a secession more or less discrediting and disabling those who remained.' Too much bitterness and fear had been spread for any peaceful issue to ensue. Besides, Newman was to say in the *Apologia*: 'From the end of

[1] Anne Mozley's *Letters and Correspondence*, vol. ii, pp. 441–2.

1841 I was on my deathbed, as regards my membership of the Anglican Church, though at that time I became aware of it only by degrees.' When, therefore, Matthew came to Balliol in October, and his father to Oxford to give his inaugural lecture in December, the reaction from the Tractarian party had begun; and the year 1842 was to see a series of defeats for it. The enthusiasm and interest which greeted Dr. Arnold were no doubt, in some measure, a part of the reaction; and, looking back, we may see his inaugural lecture as a stage in the great progress of liberalism at Oxford. In 1845 Ward's *Ideal of a Christian Church* was condemned, his degrees taken from him, the Tractarian party broken; and the liberalism which then triumphed in Oxford was a liberalism of which Thomas Arnold had been a chief creator.

But in the meantime, in the session 1841-2, Newman's position in Oxford was still secure and his following strong and passionate. No doubt Matthew heard his father's inaugural lecture and his lectures in the Lent term. He must then have realized, if he had not done so before, how great a power in the land his father was. But if he heard his father lecture, he also heard Newman preach. He must have gone along to St. Mary's in his first term: here was the other power in the land. Many years later he was to recall Newman preaching in St. Mary's: 'Forty years ago he was in the very prime of life; he was close at hand to us at Oxford; he was preaching in St. Mary's pulpit every Sunday: he seemed about to transform and to renew what was for us the most national and natural institution in the world, the Church of England. Who could resist the charm of that spiritual apparition, gliding in the dim afternoon light through the aisles of St. Mary's, rising to the pulpit, and then, in the most entrancing of voices, breaking the silence with words and thoughts which were a religious music—subtle, sweet, mournful? I seem to hear him still, saying: "After the fever of life, after wearinesses and sicknesses, fightings and despondings, langour and fretfulness, struggling and succeeding; after all the changes and chances of this troubled unhealthy state— at length comes death, at length the white throne of God, at length the beatific vision".' Besides, he would go out to Littlemore (where Newman lived from early in 1842) to hear him preach. 'Or', he goes on, 'if we followed him back to his seclusion at Littlemore, that dreary village by the London Road, and to the house of retreat and the Church which he built there—a mean house such as Paul might have lived in when he was tent-making at Ephesus, a church plain and thinly sown with worshippers—who could resist him there either, welcoming back to the severe joys of church-fellowship, and of daily worship and prayer, the firstlings of a generation which had well-nigh forgotten them? Again I seem to hear him: "The season is chill and dark, and the breath of the morning is damp, and worshippers are few; but all this befits those who are by their profession penitents and mourners, watchers and pilgrims. More dear to them that loneliness, more cheerful that severity, and more bright that gloom, than all those aids and appliances of luxury by which men nowadays attempt to make prayer less disagreeable to them. True faith does not covet comforts; they who realize that awful day, when they shall see Him face to face whose eyes are as a flame of fire, will as little bargain to pray pleasantly now as they will think of doing so then".'

III

'Who could resist the charm of that spiritual apparition?' he says; and again, 'who could resist him in Littlemore either?' But there is in all this more than a little, however splendid, rhetoric. 'Who could resist him there either, welcoming back to the severe joys of church-fellowship, and of daily prayer and worship, the first-lings of a generation which had well-nigh forgotten them?' But the answer is that Arnold himself could; or rather, judging from his manner of recollection, that there was, on his part, no call, no need, for any great effort to resist him. There was charm and there was drama. But there is not, in this way of writing, nor is there anywhere else in Arnold's writings, a hint that Newman now created for him any sense of crisis or of urgent decision. There is a savour and an agreeable relish, and there is certainly, also, admiration. But the relish and the admiration are not for what, in the end, Newman was above all concerned with. It was not so with Clough, with whom Arnold became intimate from his first term in Oxford. Clough, in his own words, was 'a straw drawn up the draught of a chimney' by Newman and the High Church Movement. But there is no evidence that Arnold stood in any such danger. After a visit to the Chartreuse in 1851, he wrote a poem about the Carthusians; and for the Carthusians we can read Newman and Keble:

> *Not as their friend, or child, I speak!*
> *But as, on some far northern strand,*
> *Thinking of his own Gods, a Greek*
> *In pity and mournful awe might stand*
> *Before some fallen Runic stone—*
> *For both were faiths, and both are gone:*

'pity and mournful awe' for something so moving, so gracious, so accomplished and so hopelessly mistaken.

I am not at all disposed to complain that Arnold did not suffer a conversion to High Church belief; that is no part of my purpose. What I remark now is his attitude to Newman and the High Church Movement which was not at all, so far as I am able to see, the consequence of the influence on him of his father's very different theology. If I am right in this, it is very remarkable. For the son of Dr. Arnold had heard a great deal about Newman before he came up to Balliol in 1841. The *Tracts for the Times* had been coming out since 1833. In 1836 Dr. Arnold wrote, for the *Edinburgh Review*, his celebrated and virulent attack on the Oxford Movement, which he called *The Oxford Malignants*, and which was called forth by the Hampden controversy. Matthew, indeed, was only 14 at this time; but the household at Rugby must have been rocked by the composition of this tremendous indictment, and something of what it all was about must have come home to the intelligent boy. In any case, throughout the years, he heard his father preach in the School Chapel; and in 1841 was published a selection of the sermons his father preached there from 1835 to 1841, with a preface, which Matthew cannot have failed to read, on the doctrines of the Tractarians. Besides, in February 1841, Tract 90 had been published. Matthew therefore must have gone up to Oxford with the liveliest acquaintance with the issues at stake in the University, and might have been expected to go up a convinced liberal theologian.

It is therefore, as I have suggested, to be remarked that, on the evidence we have, Matthew's reaction to Newman's preaching, whether at St. Mary's or at Littlemore, was not at all the reaction of a liberal theologian to High Church theology: it was not his father's reaction. It is quite true that our records of these days in Arnold's life are scanty; the letters do not begin until 1845, and the poems till 1849. Still, in the light of what we know, it appears that his attitude to Newman's Christianity was, at this time, not different, in essence, from his attitude to his father's. He was, when he went up to Oxford, twenty years of age; but it seems that already there was that in him which caused him to stand off from Christianity: this decision was taken; or if it was not a decision, this feature of his sensibility was already established in him. And this is all the more remarkable when we reflect on the impact, on Clough, of the controversies which were convulsing the life of the

University. The position therefore was that Dr. Arnold's son came to Oxford no more a champion of liberal Christianity than at all disposed to succumb to High Church doctrine. When he wrote the words about the Carthusians which I quoted earlier, the chapel of the Carthusians served to stand no doubt for St. Mary's in Oxford; but if so, it served to stand also for the Chapel at Rugby School.

IV

I turn now to another feature of Arnold in his youth which was indeed to endure, however changed or modified, into his later years; and it is a feature which may have its connexion—its deep connexion even—with what I have been saying about him.

Arnold acquired at school, and had confirmed in him at the University, a certain facetious manner and a dandyish air. At school and at the University he declined hard work, and his indolence made his friends anxious. He had never been apt to fix, he did not concentrate himself: and his gaiety and lively air gave him a taste for 'general society' where he was always a favourite; he had a turn for the social accomplishments. But he showed, apparently nowhere, 'that severe, that earnest air' to which he refers in one of his poems; he turned all of gravity into gaiety, and dissolved severity into high spirits. It is quite clear that this was the image of him which everywhere prevailed.

Now that this was not the whole truth about him is certain; it was not the whole truth about him in his young days as it was not the whole truth about him later. Still, something of these qualities, this sprightly, dandyish, evasive air he always kept; it comes out in some of his letters, especially those to Clough; it came to accomplished literary expression in the bland disdainful irony of some of his later writings; and it was always, in his maturest years, a part of his manner, which was always that of the polished man of the world. Dr. Johnson once said that it was the essence of a gentleman's character to bear the visible mark of no profession whatever; and Arnold would have agreed with him: he was always the gentleman. When he was Professor of Poetry at Oxford, to be called Professor Arnold sent a cold shiver down his spine. In the preface he wrote to the first series of *Essays in Criticism* he referred to this and said, in speaking of the lectures he had given from the Chair of Poetry in Oxford: 'Proud as I am of my connection with the University of Oxford . . . I have always sought to stand by myself, and to compromise others as little as possible. Besides this, my native modesty is such, that I have always been shy of assuming the honourable style of Professor, because this is a title I share with so many distinguished men—Professor Pepper, Professor Anderson, Professor Frickel, and others—who adorn it, I feel, much more than I do.' This is pure Arnold; and the key phrase there is, 'I have always sought to stand by myself'; so he had, and so he always would: to be a member of a party, to be a member of a Christian community, to be a professor amongst professors: this was not possible to him; and

when he used, as he often did in later years, to preach
the need for the free disinterested treatment of things
and the need to refuse to be immersed in the practical
life, he was saying something that no doubt had its own
value; but it also satisfied a deep temperamental need
in him: the need not to be committed, and to stand off,
and to keep himself to himself; to cultivate the urbane
tone and temper of the man of the world—never to risk,
to come near to, the acrid tone and temper of the fanatic.
So now, a young undergraduate thing of 20, he did not
belong to his father; and he would not belong to Newman either. He would not be Newman's man, as he was
not his father's; and the fun, the gaiety, and the mockery
were at once the means of his self-protection and the
instrument of his independence.

v

In speaking of Arnold in relation to his father and to
Newman, I have tried to set out the most important
thing: he could not, early or late, draw upon the prime
source of their power: the Lordship of Christ, whether
in a protestant or in a catholic setting. Still, what I have
said does not take full account of his relationship with
his father and with Newman.

It is clear that, if we look to Arnold's life as a whole,
his father influenced him far more than any other man.
It was his father who gave him his sense of the critical
importance of the ancient classics in education; who
made him aware that flanking the British Isles was a
continent with a civilization which excelled our own,

and that France was at the head of it; who made him believe that, above all, we fell short in our provision of education; who made him a liberal and even an equalitarian; who gave him the sense of the State as the paramount civilizing power and thus provided him with the framework of all his social and political criticism; who gave him his concern with the relation of religion to culture, and with the need for the Establishment; who even gave him his concern for Nonconformity and also his painful sense of its shortcomings. All this his father gave him; and what his father as a person was and meant to him and his generation, Arnold tried to convey in his poem *Rugby Chapel*, to the composition of which he was moved by some remarks about his father by Fitzjames Stephen in a review of *Tom Brown's Schooldays*. Stephen took the kind of view of Dr. Arnold which has become traditional and which takes no account of the love which those who knew him best felt for him: the view that he was (in Matthew's phrase) 'a narrow, bustling fanatic' without delight or tenderness. Still, the poem *Rugby Chapel* is not, I feel sure, adequate to its purposes: it leaves too strongly the kind of impression its author wished to remove. The picture contains little enough of warmth and serenity, and too much of a kind of desperate and, in the end, hopeless urgency. The poem's imagery is too often an imagery of despair and defeat; too much of the son's own melancholy and stoicism is imported into it; the gaunt and taciturn host of the poem is far away from the radiant figure which mastered his father's imagination.

I think it is difficult not to believe that there were between Arnold and his father deep temperamental differences; and the image of the father we derive from the poem is an image of inexhaustible energy, of a man precise, firm, passionate, and committed, in contrast to a son who was fluid, evasive, imprecise, and hesitant of commitment. Anger and contempt were the emotions of the elder's disagreement; the younger man's disdain would have seemed improper to his father and his blandness intolerable. Still, when this is said, it may also be said that, in addition to the gifts I enumerated a moment ago, his father gave to Matthew a deep sense of the power of religion to sustain singleness and endurance of purpose in the face of the intolerable persecution of the world; and he was ready enough, as the years passed, to acknowledge, however wistfully, the the necessity of religion. He was not himself to enjoy comfort or the strength of it; but that he owed to his father his power of restraint and renunciation, the austerity and hard dealing with himself which he unfailingly practised, we cannot properly doubt.

VI

In 1872 Arnold wrote to Newman and said: 'There are four people, in especial, from whom I am conscious of having learnt—a very different thing from merely receiving a strong impression—learnt habits, methods, ruling ideas, which are constantly with me, and the four are: Goethe, Wordsworth, Sainte-Beuve and yourself.' I observe that he did not mention his father, from whom (we cannot doubt) he learnt most: but he was writing to Newman, and his father's name could hardly take its place in a compliment to him. What did Arnold mean in saying these things to Newman? What *were* the habits, the methods, and ruling ideas?

That Arnold and Newman shared anything that can properly be called 'ruling ideas' I quite fail to see; and if it comes to 'ruling ideas' what was Newman doing in a *galère* which contained Goethe and Sainte-Beuve?— the list is riotously catholic. I do not pretend to know the answer. I have said that Arnold derived his ruling ideas from his father, which were to remain with him through life; he derived none from Newman. But he said, more accurately, at this time, that the effect Newman had had on him at Oxford, and which always remained with him, consisted in a general disposition of mind rather than a particular set of ideas. This no doubt was true; and to define that 'disposition of mind' would carry us far into the study of the mature Arnold. But we cannot doubt what he had chiefly in mind in saying this: he had in mind what he liked to call the *urbanity* of Newman. It seems a curious, and even a harsh thing to say: but Arnold saw in Newman the ideal of the man of the world: cultivation and chastity of intelligence, delicacy of taste and perception, a certain aesthetic feeling for conduct, the right union of intelligence and passion, courtesy and candour of bearing, the habit of resort to irony, not anger; all these things and more: everything that education can give a man: the ideal of the world. Thus from his father, indeed, some of his ruling ideas, from Newman a certain pervasive 'disposition'. From neither, indeed, their religion, without which, in their eyes, the ideas and the disposition could not hope in the end to stand against the passion and the pride of man.

VII

But I have been looking ahead, and must come back to the Oxford days; and we must see Arnold in his first year there standing between these two remarkable men, so deeply aware of them and so armed against them, who were to mean so little to him and so much. Then suddenly, in June 1842, his father died. 'In London', wrote A. P. Stanley, 'and still more in Oxford, where his name had always excited much interest—where the last impression of him had been one of such life and energy, and of such promise of the future—the tidings were received by men of the most various parties, with the shock which accompanies the announcement of a loss believed to be at once general and irreparable.'

But when, in 1844, Stanley published the *Life* of Arnold, Keble wrote to Newman expressing alarm at the influence the book might have. Newman replied comforting him, and said 'There is a great deal in it to touch people, but there is so little *consistency* in his intellectual basis that I cannot think he will affect readers permanently'; and then he goes on to say, with the bleakness which was so characteristic of him: 'if it is right to speculate on such serious matters, there is something quite of comfort to be gathered from his removal from the scene of action at the time it took place, as if so good a man should not be suffered to commit himself *cominus* against the truth which he so little understood'. So Newman, writing in 1844 from Oriel. In the spring of 1845 Matthew Arnold became a Fellow of the College, just thirty years after his father's election to a fellowship there; and Newman and he were fellows together until, in October, Newman was received into the Roman Church. Arnold had lost his father; and now Newman's going was like a death. 'It is impossible', said Mark Pattison, 'to describe the enormous effect produced in the academic and clerical world, I may say throughout England, by one man's changing his religion . . . the sensation was to us of a sudden end of all things, and without a new beginning.' But there *was*, Pattison says a little later, and jubilantly, a new beginning. 'In 1845, the darkness was dissipated and the light let in in an instant'. The last defences against liberalism were down. Mark Pattison was writing in his vein of bitter triumph. But listen now to the son of Dr. Arnold writing in 1869 in *Culture and Anarchy* about this event: 'Oxford, the Oxford of the past, has many faults; and she has heavily paid for them in defeat, in isolation, in want of hold upon the modern world. . . . We have not won our political battles, we have not carried our main points, we have not stopped our adversaries' advance, we have not marched victoriously with the modern world; but we have told silently upon the mind of the country, we have prepared currents of feeling which sap our adversaries' position when it seems gained. . . . Look at the course of the great movement which shook Oxford to its centre some thirty years ago! It was directed, as anyone who reads Dr. Newman's *Apology* may see, against what in one word may be called "liberalism". . . . The Oxford Movement was broken, it failed; our wrecks are scattered on every shore. . . .' '*Our* wrecks', he says—the wrecks of the Oxford Movement! But listen again to him now, writing, in *Essays on Criticism*, on what he calls the modern spirit: 'The modern spirit is now awake almost everywhere; the sense of want of correspondence between the forms of modern Europe and its spirit, between the new wine of the eighteenth and nineteenth centuries, and the old bottles of the eleventh and twelfth centuries, or even of the sixteenth and seventeenth, almost everyone now perceives. . . . To remove this want of correspondence is beginning to be the settled endeavour of most persons of good sense. Dissolvents of the old European system of dominant ideas and facts, we must be, all of us who have any power of working. . . .' He speaks of the modern spirit and applauds it; but another name for it was liberalism;[1]

[1] Arnold indeed declares that the liberalism which Newman fought and 'which broke the Oxford Movement' was 'the great middle class liberalism, which had for the cardinal points of its belief the Reform Bill of 1832, and local self-government, in politics; in the social sphere, free trade, unrestricted competition, and the making of large industrial fortunes; in the religious sphere, the Dissidence of Dissent, and the Protestantism of the Protestant religion.' These things composed the kind of liberalism which Arnold himself disliked; they were part of the liberalism which Newman fought; but it is not credible that Arnold did not know that this was by no means *all* that Newman intended by 'liberalism'.

and what was Newman doing but fighting liberalism and going back, behind the eighteenth and nineteenth centuries, to the seventeenth century, and to the thirteenth and the twelfth? But you cannot, in the end, have it both ways. It was not possible to be the son of Dr. Arnold of Rugby and a child of the Oxford of Newman and of lost causes. But this is what it was the wish of Matthew Arnold to be—and without the mainspring, the Christianity—of either. And it is to this last issue—to the resistance in him to Christianity—I must now turn. For there was another power in his life, of which so far I have declined to take account, but to which I must now turn.

VIII

It is a far cry from Dr. Arnold and Dr. Newman to George Sand and to Etienne Pivert de Senancour, the author of *Obermann*. The former of these was already in his Oxford days exercising a decisive influence on him; and in the pages of the second he was to find a mirror in which he would discover an image, hardly before brought to definition, of himself.

He had, indeed, been deep in the novels of George Sand during the years at Oxford. That George Sand went to his head is to put it moderately; and when in 1846, at the age of 24, he was free to travel, he set out to see the country-side in which she had set the novels and, still more, to see her. It was a pilgrimage of piety to the places and the person who occupied his mind more than Oxford, and more than his father or Newman.

She received him with kindliness, surrounded by her family and her friends, of whom Chopin was one. They talked about her own country-side, and about Oxford, and about Byron. They discussed his plans, such as they were. She told Sainte-Beuve afterwards that he had struck her as a young Milton on his travels. To him it was an intoxication which never left him. You can see this if you read his essay on her, in which he recounts the visit, which he wrote soon after her death in 1876.

But there was another subject of conversation between them. This was Senancour, who had died early in that very year of 1846. Arnold had not previously heard of him. His *Obermann* had been published as long ago as 1804. But it had come, after 1830, to a renewed fame. Sainte-Beuve had taken it up, re-issued it with an introduction in 1833, and declared that here was the prototype of Romantic melancholy. He had introduced the book to George Sand, who was deeply influenced by it and who herself, in 1840, brought out another edition, with an introduction of her own. She spoke to Arnold about the book. He promptly got a copy, and it was to be one of the books of his life. George Sand and Senancour were fixed together in his mind; and were to be amongst the masters of his sensibility.

I cannot now pause to speak of them at length. I say only a few things, very general in character. In submitting himself to the influence of George Sand and (through the ministration of George Sand) of Senancour, Arnold took the full force of French Romanticism.

He had been reared in love and veneration of Wordsworth; and certainly Wordsworth's genius far exceeded that of Senancour and of George Sand in depth and power. But Senancour and George Sand served to strengthen in Arnold's mind the influence on him of certain features of Wordsworth's earlier beliefs and sensibility: the strain of half-naturalistic feeling and doctrine from which Wordsworth slowly released himself with the passage of the years.

Romanticism—I am speaking now of the 'movement' which captivated Europe at the end of the eighteenth century and the earlier part of the nineteenth; I do not now speak of the enduring, pure, and quintessential thing which shows itself outside, as well as within, what we call the Romantic period and about which I shall speak later—was, in one of its many and often contradictory aspects, an attempt to confine within the limits of the natural, so far as possible, feelings which in an earlier day of European history had been sustained and organized within a framework of supernatural Christian belief. It tried to create a religion without the supernatural. Everything became in some sense divine; human nature, in proportion as it had not become contaminated by urban civilization, was seen in its true divinity; and the natural world evoked a kind of worship and provided, to the injured spirit of man, a sort of healing and saving grace.[1]

[1] This 'religion' of nature was as doomed to failure as an attempt to pour the Atlantic into a thimble. But it needs to be said that, in England at least, it had a precarious existence. Apart from Coleridge's philosophical formulations, Wordsworth's poetry is forever breaking through

This 'religious' naturalism had been nourished in Arnold by his reading of Wordsworth and no doubt of other English Romantic writers; it was already, in his Oxford days, stronger in him than the supernaturalism of his father or of Newman; and it was confirmed in him now by French Romanticism and George Sand and Senancour. This naturalism, which had armed him against the Christianity of his father and of Newman, was now reinforced in him, and was to remain with him all his days. The preface to *Mixed Essays*, in which his essay on George Sand occurs and which appeared in 1876, concludes with approval of words from George Sand which contain the heart of the matter and which he translates as: '. . . the ideal life, which is none other than man's normal life as we shall some day know it'; and the essay itself is given up chiefly to a warm exposition of her religion of nature.

But the religion of nature had, as I may say, a seamy side to it. It was bound to have. No religion is easy of belief. But a religion which seeks to build itself on human nature, and to look, for the salvation of man from his no doubt frequent ills, to natural sources, is in for a hard time of it. Any religion which is to stand, and to have saving power, must be hard-headed, and eschew easy illusions; and any religion which is to endure and to capture the allegiance of many men and many generations will make no large drafts on any temporal future. Christianity, which has at least shown con-

it; and the poetry of Shelley and Keats shows the true Romantic knowledge of the limits of the natural.

siderable staying power, has certainly not said that the ideal life is none other than man's normal life as we shall one day know it. And the religion of nature, where it was entertained by a candid and seeking spirit who judged that any supernatural religion was not now possible, was only too likely, at best, to provide an uneasy and restless satisfaction and at worst, to precipitate melancholy, inertia, and paralysis of effort. This is what we see in Senancour's *Obermann* to which George Sand introduced Arnold. The religion of nature only barely sustained him. There was, he thought, a law of his true natural being, could he but find it, could he but be himself. Somewhere, deep in his human nature, were the sources of impregnable peace and simplicity: but to come upon them and draw infallibly upon them —this was the quest. Withdraw then from the world and its intolerable distractions, and submit to the peace of nature: only in this way can you be aided to the peace that is somehow, somewhere, within you, when, in Arnold's words,

> *A man becomes aware of his life's flow,*
> *And hears its winding murmur: and he sees*
> *The meadows where it glides, the sun, the breeze.*

But in fact this less than human world is not, in the end, nor can it be, a saving power. How can it be? The natural world appears too often impassively to endure in the face of the transitoriness of human life—

> *The world in which we live and move*
> *Outlasts aversion, outlasts love—*

and only exacerbates our human distress. For the truth is, Senancour sought the infinite in the creature and what lies beyond time in the temporal. Hence the melancholy, the shifting of belief, the turning to ancient pagan philosophies, the acedia, the loneliness, and half a dozen other sides of this psychopathy of the spirit. If you persist in wanting an eternity, and must decline the classic answers of Christianity, while all the time indulging a certain nostalgia for them, you are in for all the ailments of Obermann.

And to Arnold, reading the pages of *Obermann*, here was the modern situation: it was very much his situation: a stricken, unhappy state from which there seemed no escape. This was the sense of things which is conveyed in his poetry, which seems even to be cherished there. For it suited, though it may seem harsh to say so, his temperament, which, as I said earlier, required that he remain fluid, uncommitted, and imprecise. He was not apt, his father had always said, to fix. The Obermann situation matched a certain restlessness and inconstancy in him; and his temperamental loneliness, his feeling of not belonging, and of not wanting to belong, found here both a satisfaction and a justification. Like Obermann, he would pursue his own way, a sad and austere isolation; he could only add to this, what was not in Obermann, something of the gay note and the protective mask of the dandy.

He had a way of nosing out people like himself: the Senancour of *Obermann* was one; Maurice de Guérin, like himself deeply read in Senancour, was another.

They defined for him an image of himself which he embraced with a sad alacrity. Here he is, writing years later, about Maurice de Guérin; what he says will serve as a portrait of himself: 'Strong and deep religious feelings he had, implanted in him by nature, developed in him by the circumstances of his childhood: but he had also (and here is the key to his character) that temperament which opposes itself to the fixedness [his father's word] of a religious vocation, or any vocation of which fixedness is an essential attribute; a temperament mobile, inconstant, eager, thirsting for new impressions, abhorring rules, aspiring to a "renovation without end"; a temperament common enough among artists, but with which few artists, who have it to the same degree as Guérin, unite a seriousness and a sad intensity like his.' It is hardly possible that, in writing these words, he did not think that he was also describing himself.

IX

Such was the young Matthew Arnold. It was not the two most conspicuous representatives of Protestant and Catholic Christianity in England who chiefly held his imagination now. Instead, he vaguely saw himself cast in the role of an English Senancour. He cast himself, that is to say, for a role of lonely suffering; and the manner, the airs and graces, and the banter, would act as a disguise and a mantle. No doubt he cherished this image of himself excessively; and when the days of his poetry were over, and prose was his medium, his elegiac

sadness took the form of writing about men he implicitly judged to be like himself: de Guérin, Falkland,
Joubert, Marcus Aurelius: men, he thought, who were
touched by the finger of doom, men of pathetic beauty
in the grasp of fatality. This was how he wrote about
Falkland who, he said, despite his destiny, knit his
brows and held on his way.

This then was the image of himself nourished by his
reading of Senancour; we may call it 'Romantic' if we
like; it is better to call it pseudo-romantic or even
sentimental; but as such it provided to him an assur-
ance against self-commitment, against committing himself, in Keats's words in speaking of Milton, to the
Extreme. It is this failure which we see in his poetry.
With his poetry I cannot now deal. But of all the poetry
of the mid-nineteenth century, Arnold's is, I suppose,
the best known. We all know *The Scholar Gypsy*, or parts
of it, by heart; we know its rhythms, its ethos. But
Arnold knew in his heart what its faults were, and its
limitations. Poetry cannot rest in a fluctuating, pic-
turesque dismay: it must move on, sharpen its vision,
commit itself to the Extreme, shed its protective illusions. But this his poetry did not do; and by 1855, when
he was a young man of 33, the bulk of his poetry was
written. He turned then, with a certain obstinate
defiance, to writing *Merope*, a drama in the ancient style
on an ancient subject; but this, as everybody knows,
was lifeless. The classical manner was only another
escape. The truth was that, if his poetry was to be saved
and to grow, it could only do so by a development and

extension in him of the high Romanticism manifested
in an earlier generation of English writers; but this
Arnold would not or could not see. He failed to apprehend the spiritual sources of Romanticism and its great
depth and catholicity; and in his critical writings he
proposed a view of poetry and of its role in the economy
of the human spirit which undermined its power and
authority. From the failure, or the cessation, of his own
poetry, he turned to critical formulations which both
explained that failure and provided no basis for the
future of poetry. In the fifties, which saw Arnold's
poetry ceasing, and which turned him into a critic of a
Romantic Aesthetic which he only partly apprehended,
Baudelaire, in France, basing himself on an Aesthetic
very similar to that of Coleridge,[1] initiated the most
important literary movement in Europe since that of
Wordsworth and Coleridge. It remains one of the great
ironies of literary history that it was France and not
England which, in the second half of the nineteenth
century, provided a home to a symbolist movement in
poetry, and that Victorian England failed to use its
poetic inheritance. Arnold became aware, and remained deeply aware, of George Sand and Senancour;
he seems never to have heard of Baudelaire.

But now, as his poetry ceased, what should Arnold
do? What remained or became the enabling powers of
his later life? It cannot be said of him that he came to
any true simplicity of mind. There always remained in
him something evasive and indetectable; he cherished

[1] *Salon de 1859*, iii and iv.

a number of roles; he would not commit himself with any precision; he was not apt to fix; he sought to stand by himself; there were always the airs and graces and the eye-glass. But also, there were always Newman and his father. Newman, the detailed image of culture, the 'miracle of intellectual delicacy', his fineness, his tact, his urbanity, distilling, said Arnold, the essence of Oxford's power and charm, fulfilling all that Arnold was to comprise under the name of culture; nor do I doubt that it was the thought of Newman which made Arnold so lifelong and absorbed a reader in the great Catholic writers of his own and earlier times: you have only to read his account, in the early pages of *A French Eton*, of his visit to Lacordaire in 1859, to realize the depth of his feelings for cultivated Catholic piety and how strongly he was drawn to it: so strongly that, after all, perhaps it was his father's influence which had protected him from the snare of Newman's doctrine at Oxford.

And then his father. It was his father who implanted in him a sense of a European culture, who made him, in the end, a missioner for higher education and as much of a school-master and a don as so elusive a being could be, who gave him the framework of ideas within which he composed his social and political writings, who made him eager to make Christianity, though in some false, impossible form, a power in the confusion of the nineteenth century: all this, so that, as his life moved on, we see at work in him the legacy of Dr. Arnold, secularized indeed, yet powerful, providing the chief causes and motives of his life. It may be that Arnold's addiction to the listless Senancour was in some sense a reaction from the spectacle of the matchless and confident energy of his father: the indolent dreamer of Jaman may have been a welcome relief. Still, it was on that energy and confidence, though not on their deep source, that he drew in the end. Senancour may have made him a poet; it was his father's spirit which upheld him when poetry failed in his hands, and gave him his duties, and the zeal and the austerity to perform them.

In the volume of his poetry which was published in 1867 there were published for the first time *Rugby Chapel* and the second poem on Obermann. The first poem on Obermann had appeared in 1852; it showed the Obermann of romantic reverie. The second shows another Obermann who had thought longer and more deeply; he is changed almost out of recognition; and the poem ends with a discourse by the shade of this transfigured Obermann, who urges Arnold to a life of courage, action, and hope in the face of a new world to be born. It is not too much to say that Obermann, with the passage of years, had come to acquire something of the ringing confident accents of Dr. Arnold of Rugby. It was his father who, in the end, won the day, so far as the day was won at all; the poetry was an interlude; and Dr. Arnold's son became, not indeed a schoolmaster, but at least an inspector of schools; and not a professor, but at least Professor of Poetry at Oxford.

2

THE ROMANTIC INHERITANCE

I

I HAVE tried to convey an impression of the temperament of Arnold and of the influences on him of some of the great powers in his life, his father, Newman, George Sand, and Senancour. But I ventured also to say something of his poetry and criticism; and this I must now develop and explain. I said that we see Arnold, in his poetry, and then in his critical writings, failing to comprehend the great Romantic thesis of Wordsworth and Coleridge, or at least, declining what he only partly understood. I go on now to expound the Romantic Aesthetic; and I shall then, in later lectures, try to show Arnold's failure to seize and develop it.

II

Oriel College, Oxford, in the first thirty years of the century, proved to be a spiritual watershed. Thomas Arnold, during the tenure of his fellowship and afterwards, was drawn into ever deeper friendship with Whateley and Hawkins, perhaps the two most representative of the Oriel Noetics. Newman, succeeding Arnold in his fellowship, found a common room stinking of logic, learning indeed a great deal from Whateley and Hawkins, as he readily admitted in the *Apologia*, but drawn more and more to Keble from whom he was to learn another logic—the logic of *The Grammar of Assent*. But behind Thomas Arnold and Newman alike, with all, and in spite of all, their differences, lay their common source—the huge, ungainly, indefinable Romantic epoch. Newman was at pains, in a well-known essay written in 1837, to explain that Scott, Coleridge, Southey, and Wordsworth led on to, and helped to create, a disposition of mind 'favourable to the reception of Catholic truth'; and I do not doubt that we can best understand Newman as one of the great English Romantic writers. On the other side, Thomas Arnold made early acquaintance with the writings of Wordsworth and Coleridge. J. T. Coleridge was an undergraduate at Corpus with him, introduced him to the *Lyrical Ballads* and the volumes of 1807, and regaled him from time to time with stories of his visits to his uncle. Thomas Arnold was to become an intimate friend of Wordsworth, and Coleridge was to affect his thought profoundly. Matthew Arnold grew to manhood under the power of the Romantic movement and the contradictory issues of it.

It is true that when his first volume of poetry was published, in 1849, the Romantic Movement, as we ordinarily think of it, was at some distance. Shelley had died in the year of Arnold's birth, and Keats a year earlier. Scott had died in 1832, Coleridge in 1834. Wordsworth enjoyed a great reputation throughout the thirties; but Tennyson's *Poems* of 1842 eclipsed him;

and when in 1850 *The Prelude* and *In Memoriam* appeared (the first posthumously) it was *In Memoriam* which was chiefly read. When *The Strayed Reveller* appeared in 1849, the hey-day of Tennyson's fame as a Victorian poet had begun: it was a new and different poetry which now reigned.

Tennyson had gone to Cambridge some dozen years before Arnold went to Oxford; and at Cambridge he had joined the company of young men who called themselves the Apostles. Already, then, we feel that we are in a new age. F. D. Maurice and John Sterling, two notable Apostles, had indeed gone down; but they had left a deep impression on the Society and given it a distinctive ethos and direction. Connop Thirlwall, though not himself an Apostle, represented, perhaps more than any single figure, the new intellectual interests of the University. Like Thomas Arnold, he was aware of the importance of Niebuhr, and was deeply interested in German biblical scholarship. The Apostles were well aware of these new interests. The writings of the Romantic poets provided the chief subjects for their literary debates; but they also knew about Herschel, Davy, and Faraday; and when Lyell's *Principles of Geology* came out, early in the thirties, Tennyson set himself, in some anxiety, to read it. The poetry of Tennyson came therefore, like Arnold's, out of an increasingly confused intellectual background; and science was coming, more and more, to be apprehended as removing, or threatening to remove, the autonomy and vision of poetry; the role of poetry was becoming obscure, and its authority in dispute. I am not now concerned to treat directly the great issues which are here involved: they will inevitably recur at a later stage. Still, I wish to look back now to the great Romantic writers, and to recall the way in which they apprehended the relation of philosophy and science to poetry; and I shall find it convenient to speak of Wordsworth, whose history and doctrine, in these respects, is of special importance for my purpose.

III

Anyone who has read through *The Prelude* knows that Wordsworth did not come easily or naturally to the poetic faith which animated the body of his writings. He was, to use the expression of William James in his book on religious experience, 'twice-born' to poetry. It will be remembered that he recounts in *The Prelude* the disappointment and dismay he suffered as the French Revolution took its course; and he became, to renew his confidence, a student and disciple of the philosopher Godwin. He was quickly disillusioned with Godwin, and then set himself to become a philosopher in his own right. But his attempt at philosophy was a failure. He tells us[1] that he ended up by dragging

> *all passions, notions, shapes of faith*
> *Like culprits to the bar, suspiciously*
> *Calling the mind to establish in plain day*
> *Her titles and her honours, now believing*
> *Now disbelieving, endlessly perplex'd . . .*

[1] I quote from the 1805 version of *The Prelude*.

> *. . . till, demanding* proof
> *And seeking it in everything, I lost*
> *All feeling of conviction, and . . .*
> *Yielded up moral questions in despair.*

This was the result of his philosophizing; and he passed
sentence as well, he tells us, on history and poetry:

> *their rights*
> *Seem'd mortal, and their empire passed away.*

This was in 1796. His philosophical intelligence, such
as it was, proved a dissolvent of any belief and confidence that were left to him, not only in the power of
thought, but in poetry also.

And yet, in 1798, two years later, he wrote *Lines Composed above Tintern Abbey*; and in *Tintern Abbey* he spoke
of the

> *blessed mood,*
> *In which the burthen of the mystery,*
> *In which the heavy and the weary weight*
> *Of all this unintelligible world*
> *Is lightened;*

and said that

> *With an eye made quiet by the power*
> *Of harmony, and the deep power of joy,*
> *We see into the life of things.*

I must not now recount the way in which he came out
of his philosophic despair into this poetic vision and the
blessed moods in which the burthen of the mystery was
lightened for him. I shall only say that he found what

he called the 'hiding places of power' in his remembered childhood; and that when he said that the child is father of the man he only recorded what was a palmary fact about his own poetic history. But my point now is that the renewal of his imaginative power, which brought him, in the course of a few years, to write verses that have made him the third English poet, emerged out of a time of intellectual failure. He had tried to be a philosopher; but his doing so was only a sign of temporary imaginative disorder, and served only to emphasize and exacerbate it.

IV

I have recounted this vital episode in Wordsworth's life to show how Wordsworth became a great poet only after deviating into and then abjuring philosophy. But then, when in 1800 he revised his Preface to the second edition of the *Lyrical Ballads*, he had some things to say about poetry in relation to philosophy and science. He was willing now to speak of these things out of his renewed imaginative power and vision. He speaks of the truth of poetry in relation to philosophy and science; and this is what he says: 'Aristotle, I have been told, has said that Poetry is the most philosophic of all writing.' (I intervene here to add that in fact Aristotle said no such thing; Wordsworth makes quite clear that he has not read Aristotle.) Then he says baldly: 'It is so.' Aristotle may or may not have said it; but Wordsworth has said so. Then he goes on: 'Its object is truth, not individual and local, but general and operative; not standing upon external testimony, but carried alive into the heart with passion; truth, which is its own testimony, which gives competence and confidence to the tribunal to which it appeals, and receives them from the same tribunal. Poetry is the image of man and nature.' What confidence is here! Here is the Romantic doctrine of the autonomy of the imagination, which submits itself to no higher tribunal, and is both appellant and tribunal. There is no question of either philosophy or science standing over poetry as a source of external testimony on which it must depend. Philosophy, indeed, he deals with in a summary fashion: poetry is the most philosophical of all writing. He was now, he believed, more truly a philosopher than he had been in 1796 when he turned philosopher for a time and sought out, by proof and demonstration, the nature of man, and of good and evil.

Wordsworth then speaks of poetry in relation to science, and he says: 'The knowledge both of the Poet and of the Man of science is pleasure; but the knowledge of the one cleaves to us as a necessary part of our existence, our natural and inalienable inheritance; the other is a personal and individual acquisition, slow to come to us and by no habitual and direct sympathy connecting us with our fellow-beings.' This is how he asserts the abstractness and partiality of science; its knowledge is dehumanized: it is a 'less necessary part of our existence'. But he then goes on to say this, and in saying it affirms something every word of which is weighted with conviction and urgency, and which is a vital part of the Romantic theory of knowledge: 'Poetry is the breath and finer spirit of all knowledge; it is the impassioned expression which is in the countenance of all Science.' A little later he repeats this by saying: 'Poetry is the first and last of all knowledge—it is as immortal as the heart of man.' He has said that poetry, or as Coleridge would say, the imagination, is the beginning of all knowledge—the first of all knowledge. But it is also the last of all knowledge; and what he means by this in regard to science he goes on to explain: 'The remotest discoveries of the Chemist, the Botanist, or Mineralogist, will be as proper objects of the Poet's art as any upon which it can be employed, if the time should ever come when these things shall be familiar to us, and the relations under which they are contemplated by the followers of these respective sciences shall be manifestly and palpably material to us as enjoying and suffering beings. If the time should ever come when what is now called science, thus familiarized to men, shall be ready to put on, as it were, a form of flesh and blood, the Poet will lend his divine spirit to aid the transfiguration, and will welcome the Being thus produced, as a dear and genuine inmate of the household of man.' That is to say, poetry is the condition of the existence of science and the base of its operations however abstractive: it is also the end of science in the measure that science is to be, or can be, of properly human importance.

Now these historic statements, which together make up the most important statement of the nineteenth century on the relation of poetry to science, is full of Wordsworth's confidence: it is his classic assertion, in the face of science, of the autonomy of poetry. It is not only that there is no question of the possession by science of any external authority over poetry; he declares also that poetry is the soul of science and the expression in its countenance; it is also its consummation as a human activity. It is not science which shall say what man and nature are; it is in poetry that we perceive the 'image' of man and nature; it is in poetry we really see what they are.

I do not think it possible to exaggerate the importance of what Wordsworth says here. If it is true, and if it were widely accepted, the culture of the twentieth century would be transformed.

v

In order that I may later say what I have in mind to say about Matthew Arnold, I must speak further about the Romantic doctrine of human knowledge. I have used Wordsworth as my starting-point: in what follows I shall set out more generally the essential features of Romantic thought about poetry as they appear in the writings of the great Romantic poets.

In the Romantic doctrine of human knowledge, the fundamental notion is that, in any analysis of human knowledge, Aesthetic must hold the prime place. 'An universal Poetic Genius exists' said Blake; and again, 'Man by his reasoning power can only compare and judge what he has already perceived'. The imagination is 'the living power and prime agent of all human perception', said Coleridge; and I quoted Wordsworth a moment ago as saying that poetry is the first and last of all knowledge. 'I am certain of nothing but of . . . the truth of imagination', said Keats; and Shelley said that 'reason is to the imagination as the instrument to the agent, as the shadow to the substance'. Here then is the point at which above all it is necessary to understand Romanticism; this was the doctrine with which these writers began and which sustained them in what they wrote; it was the pivot on which the entire Romantic achievement turned.

Now the word 'imagination' has at least two strong traditional meanings: to imagine something is to envisage what is not; but also, to imagine, to have imaginative power, to be a man of imagination, is to see the object in exceptional degree as it really is. We all, no doubt, accept these two significations of the word. The second was, of course, part of the Romantic doctrine; the first the Romantic writers countered by saying that any perception of anything, however commonplace, is imaginative. Identify what is common in the commonplace, and we are left with a set of measurements for the use of the mathematicians; and are these, they said, the things that we know, however commonplace? Say, if we will, that what we imagine is not, and we have removed the world from our knowledge. The truth is, not that what the imagination envisages is not; it is that, without imagination, the perception of things could not occur at all.

This was, no doubt, a striking *tour de force*. It may be that in some obscure way the origin of this doctrine was the philosophy of Kant; but there is no evidence that Coleridge, the most explicitly philosophical of the Romantic writers, or others of them innocent of a knowledge of Kant's philosophy, regarded the doctrine as 'idealistic' or contemplated the imagination as drawing a veil over the face of objects as they really are. They only said that the imagination is as indispensable an agent in the perception of anything by anyone as in the making or contemplation of an artistic masterpiece.

Wordsworth said that poetry is 'the first . . . of all knowledge'. This was his way of rendering Coleridge's remark that the imagination is the prime agent of all human perception. And they were clear that, as a primordial thing, the imagination does not, early or late, advance to understanding or comprehension. It has, indeed, its clarity and its own form of definition; but it makes no claim to comprehension. How this may be we can see from our perception of things; we can also see it by considering a work of art. The *Iliad* of Homer and Shakespeare's *King Lear* convey no philosophies. Art remains a looking or a hearing. It conveys indeed a sense of life; but it develops, and seeks to develop, no structure of conceptual meaning. The Romantic writers therefore appealed to the highest to illuminate the lowest; the farthest reaches of artistic genius employ the power active in the child when it immerses itself in the object of its gaze.

But Wordsworth said that poetry is 'the first *and last*

of all human knowledge'. What is disclosed to poetry represents, therefore, the limits of human knowledge. The knowledge provided by science and by philosophy, dependent as it is on the originating power of the imagination, cannot reach so far. It may amplify and deepen poetic knowledge; but to do so it must put on, as it were, a form of flesh and blood; its end is to be humanized by being taken into the living body of poetry. Poetry comes, indeed, to no conceptual comprehension of life and the world. But it is only a very naïve person who sees our life and the world as encompassable by solutions of scientific and philosophical problems. To see this clearly, as the rudiment of all reflection, is necessary to understand the doctrine I am expounding.

It was a natural concern to the Romantic writers to try to see the imagination in relation to the intelligence. It was difficult not to speak of these two things as if they were faculties and enjoyed some sort of existence independent of each other. But they resisted this notion, and said that the mind in its knowledge is undivided. It is true that our apprehension of objects may be predominantly imaginative or predominantly intellectual; else art, science, and philosophy could not have come to their several lives. Still, imagination and intelligence are not two parts of the mind. The mind must employ both in all its knowing, but in varying emphasis and power, and both are comprehended within and issue from the rational nature and life of the soul. Coleridge quoted Milton's

. . . the soul
Reason receives, and reason is her being,
Discoursive or intuitive;

and in the first *Lay Sermon* he said that 'the completing power which unites clearness with depth, and plenitude of the sense with the comprehensibility of the understanding, is the imagination, impregnated with which the understanding itself becomes intuitive and a living power. The reason (not the abstract reason . . .) without being either the sense, the understanding or the imagination, contains all three within itself, even as the mind contains its thoughts and is present in and through them all.' This is what Blake meant when he said that 'the Poetic Genius is the true Man', and when he said that 'if it were not for the Poetic . . . Character, the Philosophic and Experimental would soon . . . stand still, unable to do other than repeat the same dull round over again'.

It is no doubt true, and the Romantic poets did not perhaps sufficiently acknowledge, that between these two, though dependent, cognitive powers of the rational soul, the imaginative and the conceptual, poetry itself illustrates varying strengths of tension. This need not surprise us; it could hardly be otherwise. But, as I have said, the life of poetry consists in vision, not in comprehension; and poetry ideally aspires to silence, in place of being a form of utterance. It is no wonder that in this century and in the last, as, under the impulse of Romanticism, poetry has more clearly understood its nature, it has often sought to cast off the syntax and rules of intellectual discourse.[1] Until the seventeenth century, the prose and poetry of the English tongue had not fallen apart; the eighteenth century approximated its poetry to rhetorical discourse; only with the coming of Romanticism and under the influence of its doctrine, could poetry dare grossly to defy the syntax of prose. It is true that the poetry of Gerard Manley Hopkins was a Victorian phenomenon which would have got short shrift from the Victorians; and he had to wait until the twentieth century. But the clarification of the nature of poetry which the Romantic movement brought with it needed time to show itself in the form of a severe disruption of the verbal ordering of prose.

Again, we perceive in the greatest works of poetic art something of the strain with which they resist the temptation to break their silence and to speak. We feel this in *King Lear*, as in Shakespeare's last plays, where what he does comes near to being a form of allegory. These plays are big with doctrine; but it is doctrine which words cannot deliver; it must remain 'in a form of flesh and blood' and have its existence only in the body of the plays themselves. In the end, there is nothing to say. We see this again if we compare Keats's *Ode on a Grecian Urn* with *To Autumn. Autumn* is the

[1] I do not forget what Wordsworth said in his Preface about the language of poetry and of prose: 'there neither is, nor can be, any *essential* difference between the language of prose and metrical composition.' But he is using the word 'language' here in a highly abstract sense; and in the next paragraph he destroys his argument by saying that the Poet's language, 'if selected truly and judiciously, must necessarily be dignified and variegated, and alive with metaphors and figures'.

greater poem because, unlike the *Urn*, it pronounces no doctrine and acquires, through the discipline of silence, a greater expressive power.

Poetry and the other arts therefore stood, in the view of the Romantic writers, at the farthest confines of human knowledge, where the mind can have no speech. The other forms of knowledge could be, so far as concerns our sense of mortal destiny, only contributory to it. There was no question of spinning a web of doctrine to encompass our life and the world. Therefore, there was in the minds of these poets no fear of the deliverances of science, or of philosophy; there was no danger, or threat of danger, from the rapid advance of scientific knowledge. This was one of their ways of affirming beyond any doubt the rational nature of the soul.

VI

I wish, before I go further, to restate what I have been saying in the form of another of the doctrines of Romanticism. This is that poetical knowledge is symbolical. The imagination perceives by symbol, and cannot perceive otherwise. That this is so is clear from the employment by poetry of metaphor, which is its predominant symbolic form; and poetic knowledge is distinguishable from scientific knowledge precisely in this way. Scientific knowledge is knowledge evacuated of symbolism in the greatest possible degree. That is why the Romantic writers always sought to oppose poetry not, in strictness, to prose but to science.

This is familiar ground, and I need not now traverse

it. A hundred illustrations of what is meant will be found in any page of Shakespeare's writings. 'Imagination', said Wordsworth, in the preface to the edition of 1815, 'has no reference to images that are merely a faithful copy, existing in the mind, of absent external objects; but it is a word of higher import, denoting operations of the mind upon those objects, and processes of creation or of composition, governed by certain fixed laws.' And here is Coleridge: 'Images, however beautiful, though faithfully copied from nature, and as accurately represented in words, do not of themselves characterize the poet. They become proofs of original genius only as far as they are modified by a predominant passion; or by associated thoughts or images awakened by that passion. . . .' This 'modifying' power (where 'modifying' means 'giving mode or form' to the object) is the imaginative, plastic power; it is the action of symbolism.

Now this action is not, it is clear, one of comparison, or of analogy; nor is it allegorical. The object of the poet's imagination is not compared with an 'associated image'; it is modified by it. The two ideas merge or are fused, as Coleridge says elsewhere. This is the power of creative art. Indeed, we may say that the purpose of poetry is precisely to overcome comparison; it is in this sense that the intelligence must be subdued or overcome in its play; it is by *uniting* the two images that our apprehension becomes poetic and therefore sharpened. The spiritual and the material worlds are each called in for the clearer apprehension of the other; or again, many are apprehended as one, or one as many, the part as a whole or the whole as a part: it is not necessary for me to recount the forms of poetic figure. I remark only that there seems no limit to this symbolical power of poetry; it is even able to erect the abstract into a means of sensuous presentation. Thus Wordsworth liked to quote the great lines of Milton which describe the advance of Christ to expel Satan from Heaven:

> *Attended by ten thousand, thousand Saints*
> *He onward came: far off his coming shone,*

where the word 'coming', so abstract in its normal employment, is called in to vivify our image: the abstractive intelligence is employed as the imagination's instrument.

In all the symbols of poetry there is identification of the different to the end of more precise definition. As I have said, symbolism is not a process of comparison, but of definition, not of vicarious function but of development. The symbol is not something which stands for another thing; it is the way in which the object is given precision in our minds. Still less is it any form of ornament; it is a way of seeing the object, which comes to clarity for us only in the form of the symbol. And this action of symbolism was not, in this doctrine, something peculiar to poetic creation; it was the prime agent in all human perception. It may be unrecognized, or lost to sight; but it is there, to give form to what we know; and any language is a tissue of unacknowledged metaphor.

In considering poetic creation, we must not think of

symbolism as occurring only *within* the poem; the poem
itself aspires to this condition. We see this if we observe
the development of Keats's art in the last year of his
active poetic life. The varied experiments of the earlier
odes reach their end in the ode *To Autumn*, where poetry
is exhibited in its purity. 'In certain states of the soul
almost supernatural', said Baudelaire, 'the depth of life
reveals itself completely in the spectacle, however
ordinary, which lies before us, and which becomes a
symbol of life thus revealed'. When Keats took his walk
from Winchester Cathedral to St. Cross on 19 September 1821, the warm look of the stubble fields served
as a stimulus to lift the autumn landscape into such a
symbol as Baudelaire spoke of; as it was rendered into
the form of the poem, it became a symbol of life as
Keats then beheld it: the universe of Keats's experience
takes the form of the ode; prose is now wholly purged
out of his art; and the poem achieves the muteness to
which, I said earlier, all poetry ideally aspires.

Or again, we may look to the play which was never
far from Keats's mind, Shakespeare's *King Lear*. We can
well understand Mr. Wilson Knight calling the great
plays of Shakespeare extended metaphors. *King Lear* is
not a 'picture' of reality; it *is* the world of human
experience as Shakespeare then beheld it. It was not,
in any sense, a translation of a pre-existing idea of
human life which Shakespeare may be falsely thought
to have entertained. How could it be? The play was the
form in which Shakespeare came to perceive his object,
which in this case was nothing less than the quality and

destiny of human life so far as the secular imagination can apprehend them. Poetry is never a translation from prose; it is not a rendering of a philosophy; what poetry sees it sees, and comes to see, in a poetical, that is to say, symbolical, way. And as poetry does not issue from prose, it cannot, either, issue into prose. It never aspires, or ought never to aspire, to statement, or philosophy; in the measure that it does, it is, I do not say necessarily unpoetical, but the less poetical. I said earlier that we can distil no philosophy out of *King Lear*: its end is a beholding. When Wordsworth misquoted Aristotle, and said that poetry is the most philosophical of all writing, he certainly did not mean that poetry should philosophize; he only believed that poetry can show the world more fully, however incompletely, than philosophy. In any strict employment of words, philosophy is prose, not poetry, and philosophy may no more become poetical than poetry philosophical. They may not, from time to time, obey the rules; they may fail to see themselves clearly. Still, on the most considered showing, the end of poetry is not to be, or become, philosophical. Poetry must, in its scope and powers, suffer harsh limitations; but it realizes itself most by accepting them. Keats was certain of nothing but the holiness of the Heart's affections and the truth of imagination; and this went, no doubt, for Wordsworth; this was their poetic faith, to which they had every right: poetry, they believed, issued from the rational soul. But the issues are obscured if we say that poetry is more philosophical than philosophy; and we are not helped by Coleridge when he says that Shakespeare was not only a great poet but also a great philosopher.

VII

One thing remains for me to do if I am to put myself in place to speak further of Arnold. This is to consider, in the light of what I have been saying, the relationship of poetry to religion. This is, indeed, the greatest issue which confronts the literary historian or anyone who undertakes to reflect on the nature of art. I shall state briefly the view of this relationship which belongs to the doctrine I have been expounding.

At the outset of this lecture, I spoke of the history of Wordsworth's mind in the years preceding the publication of *Lyrical Ballads* in 1798. On 13 July of that year, on his journey back from Monmouthshire to Bristol, he wrote the *Lines Composed Above Tintern Abbey*, a poem so familiar to us all, but of such deep and solemn beauty, that I quote again the lines in which he says that the spectacle of all that natural beauty brought him to the mood

> *In which the burthen of the mystery,*
> *In which the heavy and the weary weight*
> *Of all this unintelligible world,*
> *Is lightened:—that serene and blessed mood,*
> *In which the affections gently lead us on,—*
> *And even the motion of our human blood*
> *Almost suspended, we are laid asleep*
> *In body and become a living soul:*

> *While with an eye made quiet by the power*
> *Of harmony, and the deep power of joy,*
> *We see into the life of things.*

Now in these lines, deeply poetical and moving as they are, Wordsworth is describing, and necessarily in less measure communicating, his experience, which we may call mystical if we will; it is a poetry of interpretation, statement, and belief. Wordsworth himself once[1] spoke of two kinds of poetic imagination which he called 'the enthusiastic and meditative imagination' and 'the human and dramatic imagination'. Of the second kind he said that the works of Shakespeare are the most notable illustration, and this means that the greatest poetic creation in our language falls within what we might be tempted to consider the inferior of the two kinds of imagination which Wordsworth describes. Wordsworth's own *Lines Composed Above Tintern Abbey* nobly illustrates the enthusiastic and meditative kind of which he himself gives Milton as the greatest exemplar in English.

Now in what has gone before, I have expounded Romantic doctrine as one in which Shakespeare is seen as representing the highest possible achievement of poetry; in his work no doctrine, statement of belief, or philosophy, can properly be said to exist; it is wholly symbolical, in the way which I tried to explain; it does not illustrate 'the enthusiastic and meditative imagination' of which Wordsworth speaks. Certainly, the *Lines Composed Above Tintern Abbey* is amongst the noblest poetic

[1] In the preface to the edition of 1815.

meditations in the English tongue. Still, having the fullest regard for it and for the *Ode on the Intimations of Immortality in Childhood*, we may doubt if in them, or in many passages of lofty meditation in *The Prelude* and *The Excursion*, Wordsworth's genius is most signally exhibited. Here Matthew Arnold, in his introductory essay to his volume of selections from Wordsworth was, I think, in all essentials right. It was in poems like *Michael*, *The Highland Reaper*, *Resolution and Independence* that he perceived Wordsworth's greatest poetic gift, his 'bare, sheer, penetrating power'; and to these, and poems like these, I would add passages from *The Prelude* and *The Excursion*, not 'meditative' but 'human and dramatic', where he delineates the poor, vagrant figures and the bleak desolate landscapes which so captivated his imagination. It is in these that poetic truth most resides in Wordsworth's writings, where he has little or nothing to say, but much to show. And in general we need to be on our guard against 'philosophical' poetry; it is easy to let our sense of artistic power, of what may properly be expected from poetry, be diminished by looking for something in it which in some vague way might be judged to be 'philosophical'. Poetry is the better in the measure that it approximates to painting and music, and not in the measure that it approximates to 'philosophy'.

It is true enough that we find, not in Wordsworth only, but in others of the Romantic poets, writing 'enthusiastic and meditative': in Blake, in Shelley, in Keats, in which belief and doctrine and speculation

have their place. 'Imagination', said Blake, 'is the
divine vision, not of the world, not of man, nor from
man as he is natural man, but only as he is spiritual
man'; and then, with his characteristic violence, 'Natural
objects always did, and now do, weaken, deaden and
obliterate imagination in me'. Then there are his
confused mythologies, of which we shall never make
order. If we turn to Shelley there is his great *Ode to
Intellectual Beauty*; and, in *Mont Blanc*, his attempt to
envisage the Uncreated in relation to the world in
majestic metaphysical imagery. There are Keats's odes,
with their dreams of Eternity, and we remember his
saying that the imagination may be compared to
Adam's dream: he awoke and found it truth. Keats is,
by repute, the most sensuous of the Romantic poets;
and then we think of *Hyperion*, and the face of Moneta,
in which Keats tries to show the lineaments of God.

But if we have regard to the writings of Keats, where
I believe the nature and aspiration of Romanticism are
most clearly exhibited, we see, both in his letters and
in his practice of poetry, the ambition to remit in poetry
what he called 'speculation'. 'Every man', he said once,
speaking of Wordsworth, 'has his speculations, but
every man does not brood and peacock over them till
he makes them a false coinage and deceives himself.
Many a man can travel to the very bourne of Heaven,
and yet want confidence to put down his half-seeing';
and once, deeply as he revered Wordsworth, he spoke
of his 'egotism, vanity and bigotry'. There is a sentence
in another letter which refers to Coleridge, and its

thought is the same: in it he refers, in a famous phrase, to ' *Negative Capability*, that is, when a man is capable of being in uncertainties, mysteries, doubts, without any irritable reaching after fact and reason—Coleridge, for instance, would let go by a fine isolated verisimilitude caught from the penetralium of mystery, from being incapable of remaining content with half-knowledge'. It is the same thought. In the second sentence I have quoted there is the phrase 'half-knowledge'; in the first the corresponding phrase (and the better one) is 'half-seeing'; and with half-seeing the poet must be content. To translate his half-seeing into speculation or prophetic speech does not belong to the poet. 'We hate poetry', he says in the letter from which my first quotation comes and where he is speaking of Wordsworth, 'which has a palpable design on us. . . . Poetry should be great and unobtrusive, a thing which enters into one's soul, and does not startle it or amaze it with itself, but with its subject.'

This is the true Romantic doctrine of poetry, which will not suffer poetry to become speculative or prophetic and an affair of belief and doctrine. Shakespeare remained Keats's presiding genius; and if we study Keats's poetry, we see him seeking to realize his doctrine. He failed, indeed, for the bigger part. It is in this context that we can best understand the failure of *Hyperion*, and again, the unblemished success of the ode *To Autumn*. But his aim was, as he said, to make his poetry an unobtrusive thing which fills and amazes the soul *with its subject*, where the subject is something *seen*.

If I have been right, in my attempt to elicit the nature of Romanticism, to follow Keats in this, we are in a position to see more clearly the relation of poetry to religion. That relationship is best understood *not* from study of 'enthusiastic and meditative poetry'; it is best understood, after all, by study of 'human and dramatic' poetry, which is the highest form of poetry properly apprehended, where something is exhibited and nothing is said.

The truth is that poetry is not religious at all. As a free autonomous activity of the soul it must remain human and secular; its end is to behold, in the form of the symbols it creates, the human and natural world; it has, and can have, no authority to do more. But then, when it has done this, it is aware, in a state of what may at best be called half-seeing, of what lies beyond the human world, of what is not human or temporal. But this, so far as it bows itself to the fixed limits of its action, it does not attempt to convey. Here it is silent because it is confronted by what is at best guessed at and is, in any case, ineffable; and with this silence the voiceless dreams which are the limits of poetry, Shakespeare's play and Keats's ode, are content. Here are Keats's uncertainties, mysteries, doubts; here are Wordsworth's fallings from us, vanishings and blank misgivings of a creature moving about in worlds not realized. But to turn these uncertainties, mysteries, misgivings into doctrines and prophetic utterances with a design on us will not do.

Here, therefore, the poet falls back; in the end the

movements and direction of poetry bring him to a kind
of defeat which, however, if he is amongst the greatest
poets, he accepts; for poetry is not mysticism nor the
poet a saint. 'It is at once', said Baudelaire, 'by poetry
and *through* poetry,[1] by music and *through* music, that the
soul catches a glimpse of the splendour beyond the
grave.' Yes, but by passing beyond it—beyond poetry,
which the poet cannot do. He must fall back, in the end,
if only to compose; for he is, by definition, a maker:
he must create. Poetry is a profane occupation, after all;
and must remain before, and outside, the temple. Or
again, we may say that, as it approaches its harbour, it
must suffer shipwreck; or again, that its true end lies
outside itself; or again, that it is an initiation only.
Shakespeare is the greatest of poets, not only on account
of what he wrote, but, no less, on account of what he
restrained himself from trying to write. The last plays
are the wonderful and unsatisfactory compromises at
which he arrived.

VIII

I have been at some pains to explain the Romantic
doctrine of the nature of poetry in order that I might

[1] Baudelaire's words are '. . . et *à travers* la poésie . . .'; the italics are
Baudelaire's. The thought is 'by going through and beyond'. I notice
that Mr. Thorold, in his translation of M. Bremond's *Prière et Poésie* (a
work of deep insight to which I am greatly indebted) translated *à travers*
as 'by penetrating beyond'. In the passage in the *Poetic Principle*, which
no doubt Baudelaire had in mind here, Poe spoke of 'Those divine and
rapturous joys of which *through* the poem, or *through* the music, we attain
to but brief and indeterminate glimpses'.

the better explain the critical doctrines of Matthew Arnold, the ways in which they departed from those of his great predecessors, and the consequences for the art of poetry which they necessarily entailed. I shall begin to do this by reviewing what Arnold had to say about Romanticism and Romantic writers.

3

CRITICISM AND PHILOSOPHY

I

A RNOLD's first critical statement was the Preface to the 1853 volume of poems. This was, without doubt, the most important volume of Arnold's poetry. It included much the greater part of the poetry which has made his fame as a poet; his poetic vitality declined from then on.

This was the moment he chose to inaugurate his career as a critic—by writing the famous Preface to the volume. He was not reprinting *Empedocles on Etna*, on the grounds that it did not satisfy Aristotelian canons of dramatic construction. He was proposing to ride a high classical horse in his opening attack on Romanticism; and he sacrificed *Empedocles*. But in fact *Empedocles* did not begin to be a dramatic work and no one in his senses would have dreamed of invoking Aristotle at its expense. But the omission of it from the 1853 volume served Arnold's turn. It gave an occasion for a Preface which would put Romanticism in its place, and was a fine piece of self-immolation which was bound to impress. He was not only preaching; he was setting an example. But in fact he reprinted extracts from *Empedocles* as early as 1855; and in 1867 he reprinted it entire, at the request, he explained, of Robert Browning, whom he took the opportunity of describing as 'a man of genius'. The self-sacrifice of 1853 served the occasion. It did not last long.

His self-denying ordinance did not in fact stimulate a Preface which takes a high place amongst Arnold's critical writings; in some respects it is plainly bad. But I wish to remark first on an interesting feature of its manner. No one, I think, can read Arnold's Preface without being made acutely aware that in writing it he was very conscious of Wordsworth's famous Preface to the *Lyrical Ballads*. The manner and the rhythms of some of it are more Wordsworth's than Arnold's own:

'What are the eternal objects of Poetry, among all nations and at all times? They are actions; human actions; possessing an inherent interest in themselves, and which are to be communicated in an interesting manner by the art of the Poet. Vainly will the latter imagine that he has everything in his power; that he can make an intrinsically inferior action equally delightful with a more excellent one by his treatment of it; he may indeed compel us to admire his skill, but his work will possess, within itself, an incurable defect.'

This is not Arnold's prose; he has not yet mastered the urbane manner. I do not say that the urbane style does not yet show itself in the Preface. But sometimes he is not in possession of it, and then he writes like Wordsworth, and the eighteenth century echoes in the style. We need not be censorious about this. But I call attention to it, because it appears, on this stylistic evidence alone, that Arnold wrote his Preface in the very face of Wordsworth's. It was a counter-statement to what he knew was the greatest single statement of the nature of poetry which came from his Romantic predecessors. And when he says that those who practice commerce with the ancients, and suffer from them a steady and composing influence, 'do not talk of their mission, or of interpreting their age, nor of the coming Poet; all this, they know, is the mere delirium of vanity', is it not clear that he is having a vicious fling at Wordsworth?

II

What precipitated from the mind of Arnold, brought up in reverence of Wordsworth, the devotee of Senancour, the worshipper of Goethe, this attack, in the name of Aristotle, upon the major poetic creations of modern Europe from Shakespeare to Goethe? What was it that made Arnold in particular, on whom George Sand and Obermann continued through the years to be profound influences, the mouthpiece of the classical, with its qualities of objectivity, sanity, order, design? I do not know any clear answer to this question. If we seek to put it in terms of influences on him, there was Goethe, the classical Goethe and (let us say) Goethe's conversation with Eckermann on 2 April 1829; and perhaps the essay of Sainte-Beuve, which quotes Goethe on Classicism and Romanticism, *Qu'est-ce qu'un Classique?* However that may be, what seems certain is that Arnold was divided within himself, tried to serve two masters, and satisfied neither. He would not commit himself to Romanticism, and tried to find safety from it in Aristotle's *Poetics*, that home of so many lost causes. I said earlier that this was a fugitive's dream; but here he is, in the 1853 Preface, indulging it to the top of his bent and giving a rap over the knuckles, like a schoolmaster, to Shakespeare, to Goethe, to Wordsworth, and to Keats.

I said that it looked as if Arnold were taking in his Preface of 1853 a fling at Wordsworth's Preface. Consider for a moment how different the two Prefaces are. Wordsworth's was a Preface to the already published *Lyrical Ballads*; it came out of what he—and Coleridge—had done in the *Lyrical Ballads*. No doubt it was a manifesto of intentions to be further realized; but it was also a statement of intentions accomplished; its temperature and passion belonged to an act of creation; it was the complement to the poems which composed the volumes, and a commentary upon them. But Arnold's Preface is in comparison an academic performance, a discourse in Rhetoric, having relevance hardly at all to the poems included in his volume, but only to a poem he was excluding, not to an achievement, but to what he judged to be a failure. It therefore sets out a wistful aspiration, not a manifesto; and sounds a note of petulant complaint and not, like Wordsworth's, a note of confident resolution. This is not indeed entirely fair. There is one poem, published now for the first time in 1853, which may be said to illustrate the principles of classical composition he enumerates in the Preface.

This is *Sohrab and Rustum*, and it is a noble illustration of them, with a clear and moving action. Still, at the risk of seeming churlish, everyone knows that it, like the Preface, has a donnish air with its Miltonic verse structure and its elaborate borrowings: and certainly in *Balder Dead*, which appeared in 1855, and in *Merope* which appeared in 1858, he did not come near to repeating the success of *Sohrab*. But I am concerned with the thesis of the Preface now; and if we leave aside its irrelevance to his achievement in the 1853 volume, how could Arnold solemnly seek to persuade us that Greek literature should provide the models for modern writers? 'The writer's attention', he says, 'should be fixed upon excellent models; that he may reproduce, at any rate, something of their excellence, by penetrating himself with their works and by catching their spirit. . . .' But who will recapture the spirit of these ancient models, I mean, creatively? We know, and Arnold knew, that only some thirty years earlier, two young men of genius, deeply addicted to the literature of ancient Greece, had used classical themes and forms, not indeed in the way of imitators, but in the way of creative artists; and the result had been failure. Shelley's *Prometheus* and Keats's *Hyperion* were unmistakably failures; but they were the failures of genius, and their new wine broke the ancient wine-skins. The Romantic modern spirit had wrestled, and only recently, with the spirit of the Ancients and had overcome it or been defeated by it, according to our choice. A due and harmonious accommodation of the one to the other had

proved impossible. And there was no need for *Merope*
to convince us further of this. We have only to look at
Sohrab and Rustum itself and turn to the famous lines
which conclude it, which are not derivative from
Aristotle, Homer, Sophocles, or anyone else, but are
pure Arnold:

> *Oxus, forgetting the bright speed he had*
> *In his high mountain-cradle in Pamere,*
> *A foil'd circuitous wanderer—till at last*
> *The long'd-for dash of waves is heard, and wide*
> *His luminous home of waters opens, bright*
> *And tranquil, from whose floor the new-bathed stars*
> *Emerge, and shine upon the Aral Sea.*

What could be less classical than that? And were such
'graceful and felicitous words and images', with an
excess of which he charged Keats, necessary to the
action of his own poem? In truth, these lines came
straight from the nineteenth-century Arnold who in a
lyric called *The Future* published in 1852 had written
these lines, employing the same imagery:

> *Haply, the river of Time—*
> *As it grows, as the towns on its marge*
> *Fling their wavering lights*
> *On a wider, statelier stream—*
> *May acquire, if not the calm*
> *Of its early mountainous shore,*
> *Yet a solemn peace of its own.*

And the width of its waters, the hush
Of the grey expanse where he floats,
Freshening the current and spotted with foam
As it draws to the Ocean, may strike
Peace to the soul of the man on its breast—
As the pale waste widens around him,
As the banks fade dimmer away,
As the stars come out, and the night-wind
Brings up the stream
Murmurs and scents of the infinite sea.

This is the same Arnold, and it comes out of the modern
Romantic spirit, with its ineluctable sense of the
infinite—

Still bent to make some port he knows not where,
Still standing for some false, impossible shore—

which must defeat the thesis of Arnold's doctrinaire
essay. 'I fearlessly assert', wrote Arnold in the Preface,
'that Hermann and Dorothea'—he might and ought
to have said *Faust*—'Childe Harold, Jocelyn, The
Excursion, leave the reader cold in comparison with
the effect produced on him by the latter books of the
Iliad, by the Oresteia, or by the episode of Dido. And
why is this? Simply because in the three last-named cases
the action is greater, the personages nobler, the situations more intense: and this is the true basis of the
interest in a poetical work, and this alone.' But in truth
it is useless to speak in this way; the fact is that Goethe
in *Faust*, Byron in *Childe Harold*, Wordsworth in *The
Excursion*, were not attempting drama or epic properly

so-called; and criticism which ignores the profound spiritual differences between the ancients and the modern is not helpful, renders no service.

Arnold, indeed, speaks of Shakespeare, the greatest of the moderns, in his Preface. But what should he say of *him*? Arnold treats him indeed with circumspection. But the criticism is clear; with all Shakespeare's gift for choosing his subjects, he obscured the action of his plays by the exercise of a gift for 'happy, abundant, and ingenious expression', and this was mischievous. This we might have expected Arnold to say; and he had no use for talk, such as that of Keats, about Shakespeare's plays being allegories of his mind. But then, when the great period of the tragic plays was over, Shakespeare went on to write *A Winter's Tale* and *The Tempest*. Arnold says nothing about these. He might have done. But what would he have said about *The Tempest* in which Shakespeare observed the unities of time and place to a purpose not at all classical? Had Arnold reflected on the last plays of the greatest poet of modern times, he would have thrown up the thesis of his Preface in despair and stopped distinguishing, in his airy way, between the artist and the man.

But in truth Arnold's concern for the Classical, which he directs here in vain at the Romantic, is itself, in a perverse way, only a symptom or manifestation of the Romantic spirit, a form assumed by Romanticism in its habit of

> *Still nursing the unconquerable hope,*
> *Still clutching the inviolable shade;*

the classical becomes only a symbol for the inviolable thing, the other, the unattainable, the transcendent; and it is erected into such a symbol only by a certain play of self-deception, and by a refusal to face historic realities. Because this is so, the hunger for the classical in the modern spirit is a useless form of escape from its own nature and destiny; and this is what it is in Arnold's Preface. The *Prayer on the Acropolis* of one of Arnold's masters, Renan, was published in Renan's *Souvenirs* in 1883, only a year after Arnold had reprinted the 1853 Preface in *Irish Essays*. It is past belief that Arnold did not read it. It is amusing to speculate on Arnold's thoughts when, on reading these now celebrated paragraphs of Renan, he cast the eye of his memory back to his Preface of 1853, then fresh in his mind from his recent reprinting of it.

I have compared Arnold's Preface with Wordsworth's. But it will be seen that, however much Arnold had Wordsworth in mind in writing his essay, he does not at all concern himself directly with the great issues which Wordsworth raised and discussed in the Preface to the *Lyrical Ballads*. He left these aside, with a note of asperity, to preach his sermon on sanity and order in poetic composition. But sooner or later, as he left creation for criticism Arnold must speak of them; he will have much to say on these things, directly or indirectly.

In my second lecture, I tried to expound Romantic beliefs about poetry; and we might think, if we are to judge from the tone of the Preface of 1853, and his remarks there on the failure of modern literature in practice, that Arnold will have nothing to do with Romantic doctrine. But this is not so. He will have much to do with it. He remains deeply in its debt. But he also departs from it. And in what ways, in what he says about poetry, he remains in the debt of Romanticism, and in what ways he departs from it, I shall endeavour to show. I only remark, before trying to do so, that we must not expect from him any clearly formulated body of critical doctrine. It may be said that we have no right to expect this from a critic; and this may well be true. But I have in mind now those features of Arnold's mind and personality which I spoke of earlier, the 'temperament' which he described in speaking of Maurice de Guérin. We may expect that he will be imprecise and evasive. He will lecture us a good deal and be anxious to improve us; but he will not commit himself too far in any one line; he will go back upon himself, and either not be aware that he has done so, or will not mind if he does. All the cards will not be on the table, as Wordsworth's were. He will not, in the end, take enough trouble and be bothered enough. There will always be a touch of the swell.

I turn now to his famous essay *The Function of Criticism at the Present Time*, which was included in the first series of *Essays in Criticism* of 1865, in which he reviews the achievement of the English Romantic writers. He maintains the attack on his English predecessors, but now in a different point of view.

III

The passage is well known, but I will quote it, in which Arnold says what he thought was most wrong with English Romantic writing. 'It has long seemed to me', he says, 'that the burst of creative activity in our literature, through the first quarter of this century, had about it in fact something premature; and that from this cause its productions are doomed, most of them, in spite of the sanguine hopes which accompanied and do still accompany them, to prove hardly more lasting than the productions of far less splendid epochs. And this prematureness comes from its having proceeded without having its proper data, without sufficient materials to work with. In other words, the English poetry of the first quarter of this century, with plenty of energy, plenty of creative force, did not know enough. This makes Byron so empty of matter, Shelley so incoherent, Wordsworth even, profound as he is, yet so wanting in completeness and variety. Wordsworth cared little for books, and disparaged Goethe. I admire Wordsworth, as he is, so much that I cannot wish him different; and it is vain, no doubt, to imagine such a man different from what he is, to suppose that he *could* have been different. But surely the one thing wanting to make Wordsworth an even greater poet than he is— his thought richer, and his influence of wider application—was that he should have read more books, among them, no doubt, those of that Goethe whom he disparaged without reading him.'

There was lacking then in Romantic writing the proper data, sufficient materials, and adequate knowledge. We may raise our eyebrows at this. Could poets of any power, declared by Arnold to possess plenty of energy and creative force, living in the early nineteenth century or for that matter at any time, lack for data and materials on which to work? And when it comes to books, are not books as much a danger to genius as an aid? And were the Romantic writers so unread? No, says Arnold, in his very next paragraph, 'to speak of books and reading may easily lead to a misunderstanding', and he acknowledges that Shelley had plenty of reading, Coleridge (who only now makes his entry) immense reading. Besides, Shakespeare, in comparison, Arnold allows, was little enough of a reader. (What he actually says is that Shakespeare was 'no *deep* reader'. How can Arnold say so? Did Shakespeare not read Holinshed, Plutarch, the old play of King Leir, Montaigne and the Bermuda Pamphlets *deeply* and illustrate, as no one else has illustrated, that it is not how much you read, but what you make of what you read that counts?) But if Shakespeare was no great reader, or no deep one, what explains, or helps to explain, his performance? Arnold must now shift his ground.

What made Shakespeare so great a writer, he says, was not books and study; it was a society, 'in the fullest measure, permeated by fresh thought, intelligent and alive': the poet lived, he says, in a time of glowing national energy and 'in a current of ideas in the highest degree animating and nourishing to the creative power'.

What this current of ideas consisted in, he does not tell us; but no doubt he intends the world of experience and thought which we call the Renaissance and the Reformation. But then, if this was so for the Elizabethan writers, what shall we say of the times and society in which the Romantic writers lived, of the French Revolution, of all that led up to it in the writings of Voltaire, Rousseau, and a hundred others, and of all that followed from it, throughout western Europe? Arnold goes on with a blandness which it is impossible not to admire in the course of being irritated by it; he catches up with our thought, and begins to speak of the French Revolution.

'At first sight', he says, 'it seems strange that out of the immense stir of the French Revolution and its age should not have come a crop of works of genius equal to that which came out of the stir of the great productive time of Greece, or out of that of the Renascence, with its powerful episode, the Reformation'; and he says, only two pages on, that the French Revolution 'is — it will probably long remain—the greatest, the most animating event in history'. But if this is so, what was lacking to English Romantic writers? If lack of reading is not the real explanation of the failure of their creative energy, it was not, either, because they did not live in a great and animating period of history. Was there not, in their day too, 'a current of ideas in the highest degree animating and nourishing to the creative power', a current which illustrated its power above all in the French Revolution, but also one without which Voltaire, Rousseau, Burke, Goethe, Heine, Wordsworth, Coleridge, Byron, and a host of others cannot be explained? But, says Arnold, giving his reply to his own question—Why did not the stir of the French Revolution and its age produce a crop of works of genius comparable to that of the great days of Greece or of the Renaissance?—the French Revolution took a *political, practical character*; it was different from the Renaissance, which was, in the main, a movement 'in which the human spirit looked for its satisfaction in itself and in the increased play of its own activity'. Now I leave over what is implicitly stated here, that the Renaissance 'with its powerful episode the Reformation, had no political and practical character' (than which no historical judgement could be more surprising), and observe that, on the very following page, Arnold says that the French Revolution found undoubtedly its motive-power in the intelligence of men, and not in their practical sense. But this is only to say that the French Revolution was a 'powerful episode' in an age which, indeed, possessed a current of new ideas; it illustrated a great movement of mind. The French Revolution was practical enough in all conscience; but it was possible only because a whole new world of thought, ideas, and feeling came about in the eighteenth century and transformed the nineteenth century. In this world the Romantic writers lived; and it was as new, exciting, and animating as that of the Renaissance.

Now if the Romantic writers failed not through lack of books or reading, and can hardly be said to have failed because they did not live in a great and animating period of history, what explains what Arnold judged to be their failure? They had not, Arnold has said, proper data, sufficient materials to work with; they did not know enough, they did not (or some of them) read enough; they did not live in a great creative age of fresh currents of thought and ideas. All this he has said; but all this he has also unmistakably contradicted by statement or by clear implication.

Nothing therefore has emerged clearly. He has it in for the Romantic writers, certainly. But he has scarcely yet expressed the emotion he feels or clarified his critical perceptions; his analysis of the cause of what he judges to be their failure is not yet clear.

IV

Now the essay from which I have been quoting is the one called *The Function of Criticism at the Present Time*; and the phrase which concludes the title provides the key to Arnold's fundamental contention in his essay. It is that, *in the nineteenth century*, whatever may have been the conditions of poetical creation in ancient Greece and in Elizabethan times, great poetic creation required to be preceded or accompanied by a powerful and sustained intellectual effort. In the epochs of Sophocles and Shakespeare there was 'a nationally diffused life and thought', and this made their creations possible; in modern times there is required what Arnold calls 'a great critical effort': 'life and the world being in modern times very complex things, the creation of

the modern poet, to be worth much, implies a great
critical effort behind it; else it must be a comparatively
poor, barren and short-lived affair', he says; modern
times and the 'complexities' of modern times, by which
no doubt he means a situation produced by great
advances in thought and knowledge, make 'criticism'
necessary, as never before, as the condition of great
poetic creation. We are therefore required to ask, before
going on to speak of Arnold's doctrines about the nature
of poetry, what Arnold intended by 'criticism' and the
great need of it.

Here is the decisive passage, from the same essay:
'It is the business of the critical power'—which he has
declared to be essential in modern times for successful
poetic creation—'in all branches of knowledge, theology, philosophy, history, art, science, to see the object
as in itself it really is. Thus it tends, at last, to make an
intellectual situation of which the creative power can
profitably avail itself. It tends to establish an order of
ideas, if not absolutely true, yet true by comparison with
that which it displaces; to make the best ideas prevail.'
It is obvious then that 'criticism' has an immense
task; and its object may not be said to be, in the first
place, *literary*; it is rather to establish an intellectual
situation, an order of ideas, and to make the best ideas
prevail. The complexity of modern civilization requires
this agency if the atmosphere and conditions for poetic
creation are to be provided. Now, Arnold says that 'such
an atmosphere, the many-sided learning and the long
and widely combined critical effort of Germany formed

for Goethe, when he lived and worked. There was [in Germany then] no national glow of life and thought as in the Athens of Pericles or the England of Elizabeth. That was Goethe's weakness. But there was a sort of equivalent for it in the complete culture and unfettered thinking of a large body of Germans. That was his strength. In the England of the first quarter of this century there was neither a national glow of life and thought, such as we had in the age of Elizabeth, nor yet a culture and a force of learning and criticism such as were to be found in Germany. Therefore the creative power of poetry wanted, for success in the highest sense, materials and a basis; a thorough interpretation of the world was necessarily denied to it.'

Now this is the heart of the matter; and throughout the essay, Goethe, with a powerful critical movement behind him (according to Arnold at least) and with a thorough interpretation of the world made possible to him, acts as the criterion by which Arnold proceeds to judgement. Therefore when, in the passage I quoted earlier, Arnold said that the English Romantic writers proceeded without proper data, without sufficient materials to work with, did not know enough, did not read enough, what he intended was, not in truth that they lacked data, knowledge and reading, but that they lacked *criticism* in the sense in which he is using the word; they fell short as critics having the resources and power to establish an adequate intellectual situation and a satisfactory order of ideas and thought. They did not reflect enough; they had a certain provincial quality; and in spite of unusual creative power, their work lacked substance and endurance; it had something premature about it. In contrast with them, Goethe satisfied the requirements of poetic creation in modern times; above all, he had behind him, as they did not, the resources and power to provide 'a thorough interpretation of the world'.

v

We must then, for our next step, consider more fully the nature of criticism, as Arnold expounds it. 'It is the business of the critical power', he says, 'in all branches of knowledge, theology, philosophy, history, art, science, to see the object as in itself it really is.' It thus, he adds, makes 'an intellectual situation of which the creative power can profitably avail itself'; it establishes an order of ideas, it makes the best ideas prevail. Now to establish an order of ideas, such as the English Romantic writers, he says, needed and did not have, which must embrace theology, philosophy, art, science, might be judged to require a philosopher; it seems to be more than can be fairly asked of a literary critic or a poet. In 1924 the late R. G. Collingwood published a book which he called *Speculum Mentis*. This essay (which I recall reading with delight when I was a student at Aberystwyth) provides a study of the nature of art, religion, science, history, and philosophy, and comprehends them within a Crocean view of knowledge; it undertakes, with what success I do not now trouble to judge, to show the objects of all these branches of know-

ledge as they really are. Now we may call Collingwood's book a critical work; but it is better to call it
simply a philosophical essay; and while Collingwood,
had he turned to art criticism or literary criticism,
might have been the better critic for his synoptic review
of the nature and scope of knowledge, we cannot be
quite sure that his philosophy would not have got in the
way of his criticism; and we should, in any case, require
someone, I suppose another philosopher, to tell us if
Collingwood's ideas were the best ideas and should
therefore prevail.

But here, again, Arnold eludes us. He has spoken of
criticism as establishing an order of ideas and making
it prevail; he speaks also of the creative power requiring
'a thorough interpretation of the world', and we are to
understand that criticism must and can provide this to
the creative power. Now I have suggested that this must
be, in any strictness, a philosophical task; and, indeed,
there are times when Arnold clearly agrees that this is
so. He says this early in the *Essay on the Function of
Criticism*: 'The elements with which the creative power
works are ideas; the best ideas in every matter which
literature touches, current at the time . . . and I say
current at the time, not merely accessible at the time;
for creative literary genius does not principally show
itself in discovering new ideas, that is rather the business
of the philosopher', who if he is truly remarkable,
Arnold says elsewhere, throws 'into circulation a
certain number of new ideas and expressions, and
stimulates with them the thought and imagination of

his century or of after times'. 'The grand work of
literary genius then is a work of synthesis and exposition, not of analysis and discovery; its gift lies in the
faculty of being happily inspired by a certain intellectual and spiritual atmosphere, by a certain order of
ideas, when it finds itself in them; of dealing divinely
with these ideas . . . making beautiful works with them
in short.'

But now, if the creative power requires ideas on which
to work, and if these ideas are discovered and provided
by the philosopher, what is the role of criticism and the
critic? It is at this point that Arnold appears to have no
answer; or at least, no answer is clear. It is the business
of criticism 'in all branches of knowledge . . . to see the
object as in itself it really is'; it makes 'an intellectual
situation of which the creative power can avail itself';
it 'establishes an order of ideas'. But if the philosopher
is the man who traffics in ideas, discovers them, and
treats them in relation to other ideas, makes them
available, is the role of criticism to purvey them to
others who may be for whatever reason incapable of
going to the founts of ideas, the writings of the philosophers? Let the critic be such a purveyor of the ideas
of the philosophers; still, he can hardly be only that.
Arnold clearly assigns to him a role of decisive importance; and certainly, if he is to be a purveyor, he must
purvey with discrimination; he must judge the ideas
of the philosopher; he must make only the *best* ideas
prevail. But can he claim, as a critic, the competence
to do this? The English Romantic writers created

'prematurely'; they lacked, through a failure of critical power in their time, 'a thorough interpretation of the world'. But can Arnold seriously intend that 'criticism' is capable of providing this?

VI

We discern here, I do not doubt, a deep obscurity in Arnold's reflections. He will not, or cannot, think long and steadily about what he is saying; and what he is saying here is no side-issue; it lies at the centre of the entire body of his critical writings. And in truth, so long as he was willing to think in this confused way, he was all too willing himself to practise 'criticism'—as that which, in all branches of knowledge, theology, philosophy, history, art, science, is said to be able to see the object as it really is—in ways that we must now regret. I do not here propose to speak of his writings on theology and religion; but in no books, more than in *Literature and Dogma* and *God and the Bible*, are the dangers of 'criticism', as he vaguely conceived it, more fully illustrated. It is well known that in *Ethical Studies*, published in 1876, F. H. Bradley turned on Arnold and gave him no mercy. Arnold had spoken, in a well-known phrase, of religion as being morality touched by emotion. But, says Bradley, it does not help us to say this, and he goes on: 'for loose phrases of this sort may suggest to the reader what he knows already without their help, but, properly speaking, they *say* nothing. *All* morality is, in one sense or another, "touched by emotion". Most emotions, high or low, can go with and "touch" morality; and the moment we leave our phrase-making, and begin to reflect, we see that all that is meant is that morality "touched" by *religious* emotion is religious; and so, as answer to the question What is religion? all that we have said is, "It is religion when with morality you have—religion. I do not think we learn a very great deal from this".' And then again, Arnold had talked about God as 'the stream of tendency by which all things fulfil the law of their being', or again of God as 'the eternal stream of tendency, not ourselves, making for righteousness'; and Bradley wrote: 'we heard words we did not understand about "streams" and "tendencies", and "the Eternal"; and, had it been anyone else that we were reading, we should have said that, in some literary excursion, they had picked up a metaphysical theory, now out of date, and putting it in phrases, the meaning of which they have never asked themselves, had then served it up to the public as the last result of speculation. . . . And as this in the case of "culture" and "criticism" was of course not possible, we concluded that for us once again the light had shone in darkness. . . . But . . . we learn at last that "the Eternal" is not eternal at all, unless we give that name to whatever a generation sees happen, and believes both has happened and will happen—just as the habit of washing ourselves might be termed "the Eternal not ourselves that makes for cleanliness", or "Early to bed and early to rise" the "Eternal not ourselves that makes for longevity", and so on—that "the Eternal", in short, is nothing in the world but a piece of literary clap-trap.' Now here is a philosopher, a critic if you will, who in his writings gave a profound rendering of the nature of human knowledge and experience—we may disagree with it—still, a rendering, of great catholicity and depth, of all aspects of knowledge. And we see him here turning upon Arnold, in all conscience, the weapon of criticism. Now it is true, as Mr. Eliot pointed out many years ago, that Bradley was turning upon Arnold Arnold's own weapons, and that Arnold exposed clap-trap enough in the social and political life of Victorian England, and rendered great service in doing so. But my concern now is only to illustrate that Arnold's confused and obscure statement of the nature of criticism led him also into clap-trap in matters of the very highest importance. The truth is that Arnold's proposition of culture and criticism becomes a defence of letting loose, in theology, philosophy, art, and history, wilful incompetence or, at best, a kind of higher journalism. He had in fact little, if any, turn for philosophy, and spoke of it and philosophers (other perhaps than Plato, Spinoza, and Hegel) with contempt; and there went along with this a certain complacency which is one of his least attractive qualities. 'Descartes, as is well-known', he wrote once, 'had a famous philosophical method for discovering truths of all kinds; and people heard of his method and used to press him to give them the results which this wonderful organ had enabled him to ascertain. Quite in a contrary fashion, we sometimes flatter ourselves with the hope that we may be of use by the very absence of all scientific pretension, by our very want of "a philosophy based on principles interdependent, subordinate and coherent"; because we are thus obliged to treat great problems in such a simple way that anyone can follow us, while the way, at the same time, may possibly be quite right after all, only overlooked by more ingenious people because it is so very simple.'[1] *His* way may possibly be quite right after all! And it is after speaking in this style of Descartes, the author of the *Discourse on Method*, which is a classic of French literature as well as one of the great philosophical works of the world! What is Arnold doing, in writing in this way, but exemplifying the philistinism about which he talked so much, and the self-will, and the anxiety to think and do as you happen to wish, which he saw as the overriding vice of the British nature? To speak thus is to reduce 'criticism' to the eccentricity, the wilfulness, the provinciality which he everywhere deplored in English life. 'To treat great questions in such a simple way that everyone can follow us,' he says; so there come, as Bradley says, the 'streams of tendency' and 'morality touched with emotion'. 'Be profound with clear terms and not with obscure terms', Arnold once quoted with approval from Joubert. Yes; but clear terms and clear sentences are not ensured by avoiding learned words.

VII

But I have said that I am not here concerned with Arnold's writings on theology and religion: I have been

[1] *God and the Bible*, London, 1875, pp. 37–38.

illustrating the unsatisfactoriness, to say the least, of his notion of criticism as he expounded it in *The Function of Criticism at the Present Time*. But chiefly, I have been concerned to show Arnold laying down, as a first requirement of poetry, 'an order of ideas' and 'a thorough interpretation of the world'. It is clear that Arnold judged to be necessary, and sought, an intellectual authority to set over poetry, a tribunal, in Wordsworth's words, to which poetry must appeal and by which it must be sanctioned. He declined the fundamental doctrine of Romantic practise and theory, that of the autonomy of poetry; and cast around, with an air of some desperation, for a master to which poetry might be made properly subservient. In the essay I have been discussing, it was 'criticism' that appeared to fill this role. But there was perhaps some doubt about this. Philosophy appeared to occupy a dubious share in the labour of criticism; but it seems clear, from this and other writings of Arnold, that Arnold looked more hopefully to the 'critic' than to the philosopher for the light which he required for poetry. But in fact it was neither 'criticism' nor philosophy which was, according to Arnold, to provide the necessary saving power to poetry: the saving power and authority for poetry, in the end, was what Arnold called 'science'; and in the fourth and last stage of our inquiry we must consider 'science' (which must govern, we are told, all departments of human activity) in its relation to poetry.

4

POETRY AND SCIENCE

I

I HAVE been speaking of Arnold's views on criticism and of the propaganda which he conducted on its behalf. I turn now to consider what he had to say about the sources, nature and scope of poetry.

His leading pronouncements on the subject are well known. Here are some of them. 'Poetry', he says in *The Study of Poetry*, is 'a criticism of life under the conditions fixed for such a criticism by the laws of poetic truth and poetic beauty. . . . And the criticism of life will be of power in proportion as the poetry conveying it is excellent rather than inferior, sound rather than unsound or half-sound, true rather than untrue or half-true.' I find this an obscure statement. Poetry is said to convey a criticism of life; but to do this the poetry itself must be excellent, sound, and true. There is a great lacuna here which Arnold never stopped to ponder. If the poetry is in any case excellent, sound, and true, why should it need to convey any body of thought from a source outside itself? What and where are the sources of properly poetic truth? But I go on to give two more quotations. He says in his essay on Wordsworth that 'the noble and profound applications of ideas to life is the most essential part of poetic greatness'. Poetry applies ideas (presumably derived from criticism as I expounded it, in accordance with Arnold, in my last lecture) to life; its application of them, however, must be noble and profound. Finally (in the essay on Heine): 'Poetry is simply the most beautiful, impressive and widely effective mode of saying things, and hence its importance.' There are things then to be *said*: and poetry, more than any other agency, says them beautifully, impressively and effectively. But is it, on any showing, true that a poet sets out with something to say, and then sets out to say it beautifully, impressively or effectively? What then distinguishes poetry from (I use the word in its best sense) rhetoric? What did Shakespeare set out to say in *A Midsummer Night's Dream* or in *The Tempest*? Is there anyone who will say that he knows? These formulae of Arnold, which in varying forms he repeats frequently, are manifestly untrue to the nature of the highest forms of poetic creation; and they are of a piece with things he said about criticism which, as I have said, he describes as being required to provide to poetry a satisfactory intellectual situation and an order of ideas and an interpretation of the world. Criticism must provide to poetry an intellectual situation and an order of ideas; and poetry must convey this situation and these ideas beautifully, impressively and effectively. Now here above all is the 'decline' to which I refer in the title of my lectures; here is a misrepresentation of the nature of poetry, and, indeed, of all art, which was bound to

have disastrous consequences: it must either arrest
poetic creation (as it did in Arnold's case) or at best take
the nerve out of it (as it did in Tennyson's case). Over
against what Arnold says we set Wordsworth's statement that the object of poetry is truth, 'not standing
upon external testimony [from criticism or any other
source] but carried alive into the heart by passion;
truth which is its own testimony, which gives competence and confidence to the tribunal to which it
appeals, and receives them from the same tribunal'.
Now this was Wordsworth speaking out of the heat of
his early years of poetic creation.

II

And yet, there was in Arnold, there was bound to be,
another strain; and when he writes in this other strain
he implicitly contradicts these formulas which I have
been quoting. I have just been saying that Arnold
contradicted a fundamental belief of Wordsworth, and
thereby did grievous harm to the future of English
poetry. But listen to him now speaking of Wordsworth
and his poetry. 'Taking the roll of our chief poetical
names, besides Shakespeare and Milton, from the age
of Elizabeth downwards, and going through it,—
Spenser, Dryden, Pope, Gray, Goldsmith, Cowper,
Burns, Coleridge, Scott . . . Moore, Byron, Shelley,
Keats (I mention those only who are dead),—I think it
certain that Wordsworth's name deserves to stand, and
will finally stand, above them all.' Then he goes on,
'But this is not enough to say. I think it certain, further,

that if we take the chief poetical names of the Continent since the death of Molière, and, *omitting Goethe*,[1] confront the remaining names with that of Wordsworth, the result is the same. Let us take Klopstock, Lessing, Schiller . . . and Heine for Germany; . . . Alfieri, Manzoni and Leopardi for Italy; Racine, Boileau, Voltaire, André Chenier, Beranger, Lamartine, Musset, M. Victor Hugo (he has been so long celebrated that although he still lives I may be permitted to name him) for France. Several of these, again, have evidently gifts and excellences to which Wordsworth can make no pretension. But in real poetical achievement, it seems to me indubitable that to Wordsworth, here again, belongs the palm.' How heartening this is! Here Arnold renders service, with his clear confident evaluation, and puts Wordsworth, lacking in criticism and reading and thought, once and for all, in the third place in the hierarchy of English poets, and amongst the very highest names in the poetry of Europe.

Now this is the Arnold in whose debt we all stand. And *this* Arnold, almost in the same breath as he said those other things about poetry which I quoted from him and which I was so anxious to dispute, said, in his essay on Maurice de Guérin: 'The grand power of poetry is its interpretative power; by which I mean, not a power of drawing out in black and white an explanation of the mystery of the universe, but the power of so dealing with things as to awaken in us a wonderfully full, new and intimate sense of them and

[1] My italics.

of our relations with them.' Now this is different, and
better, and truer; and in this strain he is at pains in his
essay on Wordsworth to decry apprehending the poetry
of Wordsworth in terms of a supposed philosophy of
nature. 'We must be on our guard', he says, 'against
the Wordsworthians, if we want to secure for Wordsworth his due rank as a poet. The Wordsworthians are
apt to praise him for the wrong things, and to lay far
too much stress upon what they call his philosophy.
His poetry is the reality, his philosophy—so far at least,
as it may put in the form and habit of a "scientific
system of thought" . . . is the illusion.' This is excellent. But I cannot forbear to quote what he then goes
on to say. 'Perhaps', he says, 'we shall one day learn
to make this proposition general, and to say: Poetry is
the reality, philosophy the illusion.' This is another
matter. But this, we see, is what he really thinks of
philosophy—it is an illusion, or ought to be judged so;
and the field is thus kept clear for 'criticism', and the
Arnolds are let loose upon the world without any
Bradleys to deal with them. But this is by the way, and
what he says about the so-called philosophy of Wordsworth is, I say, excellent. 'Let us be on our guard . . .
[he goes on] against the exhibitors and extollers of a
"scientific system of thought" in Wordsworth's poetry.
The poetry will never be seen aright while they thus
exhibit it. The cause of its greatness is simple, and may
be told quite simply. Wordsworth's poetry is great
because of the extraordinary power with which Wordsworth feels the joy offered to us in nature, the joy offered

to us in the simple primary affections and duties; and because of the extraordinary power with which . . . he shows us this joy, and renders it so as to make us share it.' How true this is! And how pleasant to read this instead of reading about poetry providing us with a 'thorough interpretation of the world', or as being based on 'orders of ideas'! And listen to him when, in *this* strain, he speaks (in *A French Critic on Goethe*) about his adored Goethe whom ordinarily, as we have seen, he rates higher than Wordsworth. 'It is by no means as the greatest of poets that Goethe deserves the pride and praise of his German countrymen. It is as the clearest, the largest, the most helpful thinker of modern times. . . . Goethe is the greatest poet of modern times'—watch this now as a fine example of sitting elaborately on a literary fence—'not because he is one of the half-dozen beings who in the history of our race have shown the most signal gift for poetry, but because, having a very considerable gift for poetry' (a *very considerable* gift for poetry!) 'he was at the same time, in the width, depth and richness of his criticism of life, by far our greatest modern man. He may be precious and important to us on this account above men of other and more alien times, who as poets rank higher. Nay, his preciousness and importance as a clear and profound modern spirit, as a master-critic of modern life, must communicate a *worth of their own*[1] to his poetry, and may well make it erroneously to seem to have a positive value and perfectness as poetry, more than it has.' What a tangle

[1] My italics.

of evasion and subterfuge! Arnold, so often a writer
with two voices, here tries to speak with both at once,
and anyone can see that the result is nonsense. He
quotes Scherer, with approval, as saying: 'Goethe is a
poet full of ideas and of observations, full of sense and
taste, full even of feeling no less than of acumen, and all
this united with an incomparable gift of versification. But
Goethe has no artlessness, no fire, no invention . . .
reflexion in Goethe has been too much for emotion, the
savant in him for poetry, the philosophy of art for the
artist.' Then, when he sees Goethe in this light, he allows
that Wordsworth's remark, that Goethe's poetry was
not inevitable enough, was 'striking and true'; 'Wordsworth is right', he says, 'Goethe's poetry is not inevitable. . . . But Wordsworth's poetry, when he is at his
best, is inevitable, as inevitable as nature herself.' But
if all this is so, was Wordsworth then the greater poet
of the two? To this question Arnold gives two answers:
the one from the Victorian critic who wanted to make
the best ideas prevail and then have them applied by
poetry to life; the other from the poet who judged that
Wordsworth, though not 'knowing enough', his thought
insufficient, 'caring little for books', created poetry
beyond the range and scope of Goethe. He said that
Goethe was the greatest poet of modern times; but in
the same sentence he explained that by 'poet' he did
not really mean 'poet' but 'man', 'critic', 'thinker';
but that being so he might have said—and at times he
certainly believed—that in real poetic achievement it
seemed to him that here again to Wordsworth belonged

the palm. This was certainly the view of Arnold the poet; Arnold the critic plumped for the 'master-critic', and 'the clearest, the largest and the most helpful thinker of modern times'.

III

It may seem very academic, or even pedantic, to speak thus at length of Arnold's assessments of Goethe and Wordsworth. But I think that this is not so. Of all writers he might count among his predecessors, it was these two who most prepossessed him: here were the two greatest, with their differing claims and varied scope, and they may be seen as standing for the two opposing strains in Arnold's doctrine which I am at pains to bring out.

Now he has said that Goethe's poetry is not inevitable enough; it has a certain factitious quality; it is more invented than natural. He speaks of the *Tasso* and the *Iphigenie* as too studied; and of *Faust* itself, he says that it is a work that, without 'a single false tone or weak line', is not a work where 'the whole material has been fused together in the author's mind by strong and deep feeling, and then poured out in a single jet'; he compares with *Faust*, to its disadvantage in this respect, the *Agamemnon* and *King Lear*. Observe that I do not consider whether Arnold, when he writes in this strain about Goethe, is just or unjust to him; I remark only that when we hear less from him about orders of ideas and the powerful application of ideas to life in poetry,

and more about the magic and inevitableness of the
greatest poetry, he sees Goethe as falling short; and
then, when he asks himself, so far as he does so at all
clearly, What in deepest truth are the sources of poetry
and of 'magic' and 'inevitableness' in it? he writes like
this: 'For supreme poetical success more is required
than the powerful application of ideas to life; it must be
an application under the conditions fixed by the laws
of poetic truth and poetic beauty'—the laws of *poetic*
truth and *poetic* beauty. What then are these laws, and
what do they prescribe? They fix, he says, 'as an
essential condition in the poet's treatment of such
matters as are here in question, high seriousness;—the
high seriousness which comes from absolute sincerity'.
High seriousness then and absolute sincerity, Aristotle's
σπουδαιότης, no doubt, in which supposedly Goethe was
in some measure lacking, and these qualities provide
to poetry, in corresponding measure, truth. Truth and
seriousness then. And these qualities he illustrates in the
same essay (*The Study of Poetry*). 'Critics', he says, 'give
themselves great labour to draw out what in the abstract
constitutes the character of a high quality of poetry'—
and he does a good deal of this himself, in all conscience.
But, he goes on, 'it is much better simply to have
recourse to concrete examples—to take specimens of
poetry of . . . the very highest quality, and to say: the
characters of a high quality of poetry are what is expressed *there*.' And then come quotations, single lines
and groups of lines, unmindful of all the argument of
the Preface of 1853 about design, order, and the sense

of the whole; lines not at all applying ideas to life or conveying what may fairly be called criticism of life but, instead, impassioned perceptions of human situations: Shakespeare's:

Wilt thou upon the high and giddy mast
Seal up the ship-boy's eyes, and rock his brains
In cradle of the rude imperious surge;

or his:

If thou didst ever hold me in thy heart,
Absent thee from felicity awhile,
And in this harsh world draw thy breath in pain
To tell my story;

or Milton's:

Standing on Earth, not rapt above the Pole,
More safe I Sing with mortal voice, unchang'd
To hoarce or mute, though fall'n on evil dayes,
On evil dayes though fall'n, and evil tongues;
In darkness, and with dangers compast round,
And solitude;

or Keats's:

Through the sad heart of Ruth, when, sick for home,
She stood in tears amid the alien corn,

—these and many others. And when he is in this vein, and writes as a poet and not as a critic or as an anxious theorist, how much nearer he comes to poetry, and how much more he heightens our sense of it and of its inexpressible value to us! But also, he does not at these times, when he is exhibiting poetry to us, quote from Goethe. From Chaucer, yes, to whom, for the most part, he denied the great source of poetry, 'high seriousness'. But, in the gallery of great quotations which Arnold provides, Goethe does not appear: what he *does* give from Goethe, with singular injustice, is a quotation provided for contrast to all the others, which is full of criticism of life, applies an idea to life, and is a couplet to the effect that talent is reared best in seclusion, but that character grows best from struggle in the world. Everyone knows that the scope and power of Goethe's poetry far exceeds this kind of thing; but, as I have said, I am not concerned here with Goethe, but with the part Arnold casts him for in the anxious drama of his own thought.

IV

I go on now to exhibit this drama in another, though related, aspect. And I turn to *The Study of Celtic Literature*, which Arnold had delivered as a course of lectures in the University of Oxford and brought out in book form in 1867: some of its pages will serve my turn. I shall not, in referring to *The Study of Celtic Literature*, speak of Arnold's at best dubious doctrines about the Celtic. I confine myself to something he says about the Germanic. He says: 'Our great, our only first-rate body of contemporary poetry is the German: the grand business of modern poetry—a moral interpretation from an independent point of view, of man and the world— it is only German poetry, Goethe's poetry, that has, since the Greeks, made much way with. Campbell's power of style, and the natural magic of Keats and

Wordsworth, and Byron's titanic personality, may be wanting to this poetry; but see what it has accomplished without them!' He then speaks of Dante and Shakespeare, and says that they erected their creations on the basis of a traditional religion; he goes on: 'But when Goethe came, Europe had lost her basis of spiritual life; she had to find it again; Goethe's task was, the inevitable task for the modern poet henceforth is . . . to interpret human life afresh, and to supply a new spiritual basis to it. This is not only a work for style, elegance, charm, poetry; it is a work for science; and the scientific, serious, German spirit, not carried away by this and that intoxication of ear, and eye, and self-will, has peculiar aptitudes for it'—that is, for 'science', where, by 'science' he does not, of course, mean 'science' as we now ordinarily understand it; he means *Wissenschaft*, that is, as he says elsewhere, 'knowledge systematically pursued and prized in and for itself', knowledge objectively and critically sought as the German universities came to conceive it in the eighteenth century and to pursue it in the nineteenth, whether the knowledge be 'humanistic' or 'scientific' as we in this country traditionally employ this last term. Goethe's poetry then was informed by 'science'. It lacked indeed style of the highest kind: Goethe's style, says Arnold, is the style of prose as much as of poetry: it is lucid, harmonious, earnest, eloquent; but it has not received that peculiar kneading and recasting which is observable in the style of Shakespeare, Milton, and others. We may then fairly interpret him as saying that Goethe is a classic of European prose; he was a re-interpreter of human life, who devised for and brought to poetry a new intellectual situation, a new and thorough interpretation of the world. But this was a work of science and of prose. Arnold has indeed implied this in quotations I have given earlier where, I said, he was sitting sublimely on a fence; but now he is off the fence. Goethe is a classic of European prose! His place is chiefly in the history of European 'science' and 'thought'! And yet, in the essay on Heine, published in the first series of *Essays in Criticism* in 1865, he had written: 'Wordsworth, Scott, and Keats have left admirable works; far more solid and complete works than those which Byron and Shelley have left. But their works have this defect—they do not belong to that which is the main current of the literature of modern epochs, they do not apply modern ideas to life; they constitute therefore, *minor currents*. . . .' Wordsworth and Keats minor currents in European literature! Where, therefore, are we coming to? Goethe, 'our greatest modern poet' (as Arnold has called him) wrote 'in a style of prose as much as of poetry'; and Wordsworth, a greater poet than Goethe (as Arnold has declared) a minor current in European literature! The drama of Arnold's swaying and conflicting thought takes on the air and manner of a fantastic comedy. How can it end?

v

To explain further all that is involved here, I turn to speak now of what Arnold wrote about the English

Augustans. What he had to say about the English Romantics I have reviewed earlier; what he said about the English Augustans is no less interesting and no less famous.

'We are to regard Dryden as the puissant and glorious founder, Pope as the splendid high priest, of our age of prose and reason, of our excellent and indispensable eighteenth century. For the purposes of their mission and destiny their poetry, like their prose, is admirable.'[1] He goes on to say of their poetry (after giving, I must say, two singularly ill-chosen and unfair quotations from their poetry) that it is 'admirable for the purposes . . . of an age of prose and reason. . . . Do you ask me whether the application of ideas to life in the verse of these men, often a powerful application, no doubt, is a powerful *poetic* application?' (Remark his saying here '*poetic*' application—he himself italicizes the word, and thus effects a subtle shift of emphasis.) 'Do you ask me whether the poetry of these men has either the matter or the inseparable manner of such an adequate poetic criticism; whether it has the accent of

Absent thee from felicity awhile . . .

I answer: It has not, and cannot have them; it is the poetry of the builders of an age of prose and reason. . . . Dryden and Pope are not classics of our poetry; they are classics of our prose.' So, he writes down the poetry of the late seventeenth and eighteenth centuries. But all

[1] *The Study of Poetry.*

this is very near to, if not identical with, what he said about Goethe, whose labour was one of science, whose style was as much of prose as of poetry, and had not the peculiar kneading and re-casting which is observable in the style of Shakespeare and others. This is why I ventured to interpret Arnold, I do not think unjustly, as saying in effect that Goethe is a classic of our European prose.

Arnold develops further, in his essay on Gray, what he says about the Augustans in the essay (published in the same year, 1880) from which I have just been quoting. 'The difference between genuine poetry and the poetry of Dryden, Pope and all their school, is briefly this: their poetry is conceived and composed in their wits, genuine poetry is conceived and composed in the soul. The difference between the two kinds of poetry is immense'; the former kind is 'often eloquent, and always, in the hands of such masters as Dryden and Pope, clever; but it does not take us much below the surface of things, it does not give us the emotion of seeing things in their truth and beauty. The language of genuine poetry, on the other hand, is the language of one composing with his eye on the object; its evolution is that of a thing which has been plunged in the poet's soul until it comes forth naturally and necessarily.' That is it; it is not contrived, not invented; it is natural and necessary; if it does not come as naturally as leaves to a tree, Keats said of poetry, it had better not come at all.

VI

The issue then is now clear. I have talked of Goethe and Wordsworth as the protagonists in the drama of Arnold's mind. But let us now turn from flesh and blood to the greater lucidity of abstractions. The issue is between science and poetry. On the one side is 'science' (which turns out to be little different from 'criticism'); prose (even when in the form of verse); thorough interpretations of the world, orders of ideas; criticism of life. On the other is poetry, its style 'kneaded, heightened, and re-cast', with the object not analytically treated but plunged into the poet's soul until it comes forth naturally and necessarily; composition in the soul, that is, by the entire and unified faculties of the personality; the imaginative power. I only remind you that I use 'science' here in Arnold's sense, not as specifically signifying the physical and biological sciences; they are but a part of the wider operations of 'science' interpreted as *Wissenschaft*. When it came to the physical and biological sciences, Arnold stood firm. 'The interpretations of science do not give us this intimate sense of objects as the interpretations of poetry give it; they appeal to a limited faculty, and not to the whole man. It is not Linnaeus or Cavendish or Cuvier who gives us the true sense of animals, or water, or plants, who seizes their secret for us, who make us participate in their life; it is Shakespeare with his

daffodils
That come before the swallow dares, and take
The winds of March with beauty;

it is Wordsworth with the

> *voice . . . heard*
> *In spring-time from the cuckoo-bird*
> *Breaking the silence of the seas*
> *Among the farthest Hebrides;*

it is Keats with his

> *moving waters at their priestlike task*
> *Of pure ablution round Earth's human shores. . . .'*

Here, at least, he seems to have no doubts, no reservations; but it is different with what, in a wider sense, he calls 'science'; and in *The Study of Celtic Literature*, as we have seen, he extols science of this order: science 'leading us at last, though slowly, and not by the most brilliant road' (what is 'the most brilliant road'?) 'out of the bondage of the humdrum and common, into the better life'. Science then shall guide and rule us, 'the idea of science', as he says 'governing all departments of human activity', and a habit of mind possess us that 'leads at last to science, up to the comprehension and interpretation of the world'. And then we are back with Goethe, and we are told that 'our great, our only first-rate body of contemporary poetry is the German; the grand business of modern poetry—a moral interpretation, from an independent point of view' (whatever that may be!) 'of man and the world—it is only German poetry, Goethe's poetry, that has, since the Greeks, made much way with'; and so we are back in the old round, the old unsolved tangle of which we become so weary. But if the Germans and the Germanic give us science, the idea of science as governing all departments of human activity and as providing comprehension and interpretation of the world, where shall we look for that highest poetry, which the Germans, including Goethe, were lacking in? Arnold replies: 'At last one turns round and looks westward. Everything is changed. Over the mouth of the Conway and its sands is the eternal softness and mild light of the west; the low line of the mystic Anglesey, and the precipitous Penmaen-mawr, and the great group of Carnedd Llewelyn and Carnedd Dafydd and their brethren fading away, hill behind hill, in an aerial haze, make the horizon; between the foot of Penmaenmawr and the bending coast of Anglesey, the sea, a silver stream, disappears one knows not whither. On this side, Wales—Wales, where the past still lives, where every place has its tradition, every name its poetry, and where the people, the genuine people, still knows this past, this tradition, this poetry, and lives with it, and clings to it. . . .' Well, the names do not matter: Goethe and Wordsworth, Science and Poetry, the Germanic and the Celtic: it is all the same. We can add, if we like, but it does not greatly help, English Dr. Arnold and Matthew's gentle Cornish mother.

VII

But now, if the unresolved antithesis is that of science and poetry, what more can we say of science, the power that must govern all departments of human activity including, we must suppose, poetry? Poetry we know,

in Homer, Virgil, Dante, Shakespeare, Milton, Wordsworth. Where shall we find science, and the comprehension and the interpretation of the world for which
no doubt we all long? Is science only another name for
philosophy, and shall we look to Plato and Descartes
and Spinoza and Kant? Ah! no; philosophy is an
illusion. 'Perhaps one day we shall learn to make this
proposition general, and to say: Poetry is the reality,
philosophy the illusion.' But if poetry is after all the
reality, is science also an illusion? Will he say so—this
vague thing called science, which is not poetry and
not philosophy and not the sciences, but is sometimes, or often, called by the name of criticism and
which must govern all departments of human activity?
No, this he cannot say: it alone can give us a comprehension and interpretation of the world—there, after
all, is the reality. What then does science give us? What
comprehension and interpretation of the world does it
provide to us, in our longing for the light? What did
the greatest of all men of science, Goethe, give us for an
interpretation of the world? Ah! says Arnold, a 'profound imperturbable naturalism'.[1] An imperturbable
naturalism! Is this then the last word of science, to dig
ourselves into a naturalism and to refuse to be dis-
lodged from it? Is this the thorough interpretation of
the world which science, or criticism, must provide to
poetry? So it would appear: and we think of George
Sand's sentence which Arnold liked to quote approv-
ingly: 'The ideal life is none other than man's normal

[1] *Heinrich Heine.*

life as we shall some day know it.' This then is what science discloses to us, and this, scientific criticism approves and must transmit to poetry; the required order of ideas and the best ideas, made to prevail, are shut within a circle of naturalism. But in truth is science, the nature of which is, on Arnold's showing, so dark and obscure to us—not philosophy, and not poetry, and not the sciences—itself beyond and above criticism? and who will properly and confidently declare that its sovereignty over 'all departments of human activity' is absolute? Who gave its throne to this shape of thought—

> *If shape it might be call'd that shape had none*
> *Distinguishable in member, joynt, or limb,*
> *Or substance might be call'd that shadow seem'd,*
> *For each seem'd either?*

Still, with it must lie the future: it alone can and must govern all departments of human activity. Poetry, he sometimes says, is the reality; but he does not mean it. How can he? And religion must be shut out, must it not, by our imperturbable naturalism? But even here he tried to find a comfort, and only plunges into the anguish of palpable and pathetic contradiction. 'The future of poetry is immense, because in poetry, where it is worthy of its high destinies, our race, as time goes on, will find an ever surer and surer stay. There is not a creed which is not shaken, not an accredited dogma which is not shown to be questionable. . . . Our religion has materialised itself in the fact, and now the fact is failing it. But for poetry the idea is everything; the rest is a world of illusion, of divine illusion. Poetry attaches its emotion to the idea; the idea *is* the fact. The strongest part of our religion today is its unconscious poetry.' Poetry then becomes religion, which, I have said, it cannot do; but then, in any case, poetry, as one of the 'departments of human activity', is, we must suppose, in spite of all Arnold's subterfuge and evasion, his turns and shifts, governed by 'science' which, we are given to understand, consists in an imperturbable naturalism. Once, in his exasperating way, he quoted with approval Wordsworth's saying that poetry is the expression which is in the countenance of all science and the breath and finer spirit of all knowledge (though here he left out the 'all'); and once he spoke of the imaginative reason as that by which we must live, and this sounds like Coleridge. But he understood neither Wordsworth nor Coleridge when they spoke like this; and this is clear from all I have been saying. The spiritual unity proclaimed by the great Romantic writers is broken in his hands. Poetry and science, imagination and thought, knowledge and being, fall apart, and no centre is left.

VIII

How dark and melancholy a scene, then, are we left with! This tangle and disorder of the mind deepens with every step: half-thought and half-contradiction follow on one another, and, in the end, nothing is clear. Arnold spent perhaps the greatest part of his energies in his role as a propagandist for what he called culture.

But in fact what we see in the pages I have been review-ing is a late stage in the dissolution of a culture, and a condition in which no pattern of knowledge and ex-perience appears.

I said that the greater part of his poetry was written by 1855. With his Preface of 1853 he had embarked on his career as a critic; and his critical writings, which I have been reviewing, we may see as a commentary on his poetry and as explaining its desolation. Arnold's poetry, the poetry we all know almost by heart, is elegiac. There are the narrative poems; but, with the exception of *Sohrab* they do not hit the mark. He longed to create in narrative and drama, but he failed: it would not do. And then we have the essential Arnold, the elegiast: *The Scholar Gipsy, Dover Beach, A Summer Night, Memorial Verses, Rugby Chapel, The Buried Life, Thyrsis*; and their theme is always the same, and it is always himself, a spirit which can see no clear source of certitude or authority, and can find no way.

> *But often, in the world's most crowded streets,*
> *But often, in the din of strife,*
> *There rises an unspeakable desire*
> *After the knowledge of our buried life;*
> *A thirst to spend our fire and restless force*
> *In tracking out our true, original course;*
> *A longing to inquire*
> *Into the mystery of this heart which beats*
> *So wild, so deep in us—to know*
> *Whence our lives come and where they go.*

And many a man in his own breast then delves,
But deep enough, alas! none ever mines.
And we have been on many thousand lines,
And we have shown, on each, spirit and power;
But hardly have we, for one little hour,
Been on our own line, have we been ourselves—
Hardly had skill to utter one of all
The nameless feelings that course through our breast,
But they course on for ever unexpress'd.
And long we try in vain to speak and act
Our hidden self, and what we say and do
Is eloquent, is well—but 'tis not true!
And then we will no more be rack'd
With inward striving, and demand
Of all the thousand nothings of the hour
Their stupefying power;
Ah yes, and they benumb us at our call!
Yet still, from time to time, vague and forlorn,
From the soul's subterranean depth upborne
As from an infinitely distant land,
Come airs, and floating echoes, and convey
A melancholy into all our day.

He was 30 then. In 1861, on the death of Clough, with
whom he had been so intimate and who was so like
himself, he was moved to write *Thyrsis.*

So, some tempestuous morn in early June,
When the year's primal burst of bloom is o'er,
Before the roses and the longest day—
When garden-walks and all the grassy floor

With blossoms red and white of fallen May
And chestnut-flowers are strewn—
So have I heard the cuckoo's parting cry,
From the wet field, through the vext garden-trees,
Come with the volleying rain and tossing breeze:
The bloom is gone, and with the bloom go I!

I said in my first lecture that, as the poetry faltered and then ceased, in early June, before the roses and the longest day, the spirit of his father upheld him and helped him to fill and moralize his days with a succession of tasks. 'For fifteen years', he wrote of his father in *Rugby Chapel* in 1867,

We who till then in thy shade
Rested as under the boughs
Of a mighty oak, have endured
Sunshine and rain as we might,
Bare, unshaded, alone,
Lacking the shelter of thee;

and we cannot doubt that the zeal of his father's house sustained him to the end, gave him the courage and the seriousness and the intensity to which he added his own uncomfortable sadness. He never lost the old unquiet breast

Which neither deadens into rest,
Nor ever feels the fiery glow
That whirls the spirit from itself away,
But fluctuates to and fro,
Never by passion quite possess'd
And never quite benumb'd by the world's sway;

nor what went with it, the dandyish, aristocratic air.

There were then two Arnolds. The first was actuated by his father to promote culture, education, democracy, liberalism; unremitting in the performance of his duty, dealing hardly with himself, the public servant. In the discharge of this public duty he manifested, what he did not derive from his father, a manner gay, mocking, bland, ironical, disdainful, exasperating, impeccable, aristocratic; and this air, this idiom, connects the public figure with the other Arnold, for which it was a protective mask, and which he poured into the poetry which, however, he failed to sustain as the years passed by. This other life, the life of the poet, was secret, fugitive, lonely and inviolable. Above all, it was lonely.

> *Who order'd, that their longing's fire*
> *Should be, as soon as kindled, cool'd?*
> *Who renders vain their deep desire?—*
> *A God, a God, their severance ruled!*
> *And bade betwixt their shores to be*
> *The unplumb'd, salt, estranging sea.*

'I have always sought to stand by myself', he said. But in truth his standing alone was not a policy; it was a destiny from which he could not escape. He accepted it indeed, and came to terms with it. But it was the ultimate cause of all his sadness. He clung, as part of the ineluctable idiom of his life, to a certain isolation of himself; but in the end it became a certain isolation from life itself. This he knew, and he was helpless to change it.

And this lonely Arnold, naturally deeply spiritual, having a feeling for refinement and distinction of the spirit, but sickened and increasingly sickened by the world around him, sought for the sources of light and truth and peace, and persuaded himself that they were to be found in liberalism, in science, and in an imperturbable naturalism. But here they were *not* to be found; and this he knew, and also, in his endless perplexity, refused to acknowledge—except indeed in such poems as he wrote from time to time as the darkening years went by; and in *Dover Beach*, which was published as late as 1867, he said that the world,

> *which seems*
> *To lie before us like a land of dreams,*
> *So various, so beautiful, so new,*
> *Hath really neither joy, nor love, nor light,*
> *Nor certitude, nor peace, nor help for pain;*
> *And we are here as on a darkling plain*
> *Swept with confused alarms of struggle and flight,*
> *Where ignorant armies clash by night.*

This despair showed itself when, from time to time in the later years, he composed poetry; he never allowed it to show in the prose, where he kept up the mocking air and the confident manner.

These were the two Arnolds, the Arnold of the prose, the devotee of science and liberalism and Goethe, the public Arnold; and the poet moved only to poetry in order to utter his grief and loss of hope. And this loss of hope, with the accompanying drying up within him of the sources of poetry, came directly, it has been my purpose to try to show, from his failure to trust the genius of poetry and its power of truth, which had been the heritage to him of his great predecessors.

IX

I have spoken of Arnold's temperament. Not apt to fix, his father said; a temperament 'which opposed itself to the fixedness of a religious vocation, or to any vocation of which fixedness is an essential attribute', he himself said of de Guérin, and implicitly, we may say of himself. Poetry is itself a vocation 'of which fixedness is an essential attribute'; and in poetry he was not able to repose the necessary faith. This failure of decisiveness, commitment and steadfastness shows itself, as I have been at pains to show, throughout his intellectual life; and indeed, he made it one of the themes of his poetry. Falling, or half-falling away from poetry, he was too much a light half-believer in his alternative creeds, obscure, ill-conceived and self-contradictory as they often were. No doubt it is easy for us to say so, too easy, out of our own indecisiveness. Certainly, because of the confusion and dissolving culture of the nineteenth century, we may and ought to forgive him much; and he paid for his indecisiveness and casualness in suffering and dismay. But in making these things the subject of much of his poetry, he did not also give his poetry an active, purgative power: it did not cleanse his bosom of his perilous stuff; he could not make it a means of discovery; it was a resort merely; and his

temperament too often falsified what he wrote. I quoted
earlier one of the stanzas from the *Grande Chartreuse*:

> *Not as their friend, or child, I speak!*
> *But as, on some far northern strand,*
> *Thinking of his own Gods, a Greek*
> *In pity and mournful awe might stand*
> *Before some fallen Runic stone—*
> *For both were faiths, and both are gone.*

Then follows this stanza:

> *Wandering between two worlds, one dead,*
> *The other powerless to be born,*
> *With nowhere yet to rest my head,*
> *Like these, on earth I wait forlorn.*
> *Their faith, my tears, the world deride—*
> *I come to shed them at their side.*

But in fact, the one world was not dead, and the other
had not been powerless to be born. The world represented by the Carthusians, Newman, yes and by his
father (who had planted in him 'strong and deep
religious feelings' and developed them 'by all the circumstances of his childhood') was certainly not dead;
and he could not truly say that that world evoked from
him only 'pity and mournful awe'. As for the other
world—the world which issued from a profound and
imperturbable naturalism and which sees the ideal life
as none other than man's normal life as we shall some
day know it—it had come to vigorous life and showed
every prospect of continuing vigour. In truth, the dead
and unborn worlds composed a piece of myth-making

which showed only Arnold's uncertainties, unfixedness, indecisiveness. As a rendering of history it was manifestly untrue; as a rendering of Arnold's mind and the spiritual homelessness which something in him drove him to cherish, it had its validity. He could not make up his mind or commit himself; he was the slave, in the end, of his temperament; and I have tried to show from his prose-writings the subtle shifts and turns of thought by which he avoided the great issues and sought to rest in unresolved contradictions. 'The longer I live', he once quoted from de Guérin, '. . . the more does the inclination to live . . . as a solitary man on the frontiers of society, on the outskirts of the world, gain and grow in me. The birds come and go, and make nests around our habitations, they are fellow-citizens of our farms and hamlets with us; but they take their flight in a heaven which is boundless. . . . So would I, too, live, hovering round society, and having always at my back a field of liberty vast as the sky.' There is much of Arnold too in all this. But in fact the 'vast field of liberty' proved a prison from which there was no escape. It was all very well to preach the free disinterested play of mind and detachment from practice; but the culture and education which he invoked were in truth etiolated things, without substance or power. They were only an escape from commitment and an aid to his isolation, giving an appearance of freedom only, and without its reality, which, being what he was, he could have found only in and through poetry.

PRINTED IN GREAT BRITAIN
AT THE UNIVERSITY PRESS, OXFORD
BY VIVIAN RIDLER
PRINTER TO THE UNIVERSITY